PRAISE FO

Allowances, Dollars & Sense

"It's an easy-to-read book, suitable for kids of all ages as well as their parents.... A worthwhile buy, sure to be dog-eared from constant reference."

—*Alan Caplan*, EDMONTON JOURNAL

"Paul Lermitte is teaching parents how to keep their children laughing to the bank for a lifetime."

—*Kim Hanson*, NATIONAL POST

"In a nutshell, [Paul's] book helps parents instill basic savings and spending skills in their kids.... He's loaded the book with tips and teaching aids."

—*Tony Wanless*, FINANCIAL POST

"Certified financial planner Paul Lermitte has made it his life mission to help families manage their money and protect wealth."

—GLOBE AND MAIL

Allowances, Dollars & Sense

A Proven System for Teaching Your Kids About Money

Paul W. Lermitte

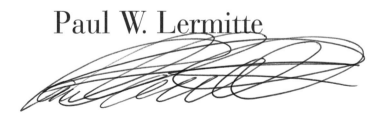

Kiangle Communications Inc.
Vancouver, BC Canada
www.paullermitte.com
paul@paullermitte.com

Cover, illustrations and text design: Jan Perrier, Perrier Design

Author photo: Dina Goldstein

Editing: Jan Lermitte and Naomi Pauls

Indexing: Naomi Pauls, Paper Trail Publishing

Library and Archives Canada Cataloguing in Publication
Lermitte, Paul W.
    Allowances, dollars and sense : a proven system for teaching your kids about money / Paul W. Lermitte. — 2nd ed.
Includes index.
Issued also in electronic formats.
ISBN 978-0-9878076-0-1
    1. Children--Finance, Personal. I. Title.
HG179.L47 2011   332.0240083   C2011-907169-

XTypeset in 11 point Berthold Akzidenz Grotesk Regular on 60lb. #2 Husky FSC offset paper.

MIX
Paper from responsible sources
FSC
www.fsc.org   FSC® C016245

Printed in Canada by Friesens

Contents

To all parents who want their children
to be skilled in money management
and confident in their decision-making.

Preface to Second Edition

MUCH HAS CHANGED in the lives of both children and parents in the dozen years since this book was first published. Whether texting friends, reading e-books, playing games, or watching TV, we all spend a lot more time "onscreen." The greater influence of electronics in children's daily lives—even the lives of very young children—means they are influenced to a much greater degree by advertising, target marketing, and consumerism. In such a world, financial literacy becomes even more important, which is why I chose to update and republish this essential guide for parents.

While kids today may spend more time hanging out online than hanging around at the playground, there are certain things that remain the same for today's busy families. Parents still seek to impart their core values to their children. They want to have a supportive influence over their kids—and counter some of the negative effects of our Internet age and consumer-driven society.

Of course, important values include those to do with money. That is where *Allowances, Dollars & Sense* can help. By setting out a simple system to teach your children money management skills, it also gets your family talking and thinking about money— and your own money values. This book makes your job as a parent easier and ensures you cover all the basics.

Readers familiar with the first edition of this book may notice that this one is a little slimmer. To benefit time-strapped parents, it concentrates on the core lessons about money for children age six to twelve, including weekly allowance, saving basics, and property values. (No worries, these lessons can also be adapted for teens.) A subsequent book will address money issues for older kids, such as understanding credit, learning about investments, and making independent choices. Stay tuned for future books in the Family Finances series geared specifically to young adults and to family business owners dealing with succession.

Money management is a serious business, but teaching your children about money is both worthwhile and rewarding. When you see your kids save for their first big purchase or demonstrate on their own initiative the "gift of giving," your heart will brim with pride and satisfaction. I hope this book helps to make your own family's journey to financial literacy a rich and enjoyable experience. Times change, and with the pace of technological advances, we cannot predict what forms money will take in the future. However, we know money management will always be an essential skill—for children, for their parents, and for all families.

Acknowledgments

FOR THEIR HELP on this second edition, I would like to thank my "dream team," Naomi, Erin Anne, and Jan, who ably demonstrated their expertise, teamwork, and willingness to stretch one another to see the project completed. Their vision of what the book could be was valuable and inspiring.

Secondly, I want to thank my wife, Jan, who has partnered with me to raise our kids and to make these book projects a reality. With her master's in English literature, she is my own brilliant in-house editor. Her editorial feedback helped me to retain the essence of who I am in the book.

Over the years, many family members, friends, and colleagues have shared their own family and business stories, and encouraged me and provided feedback on this project. I offer them my thanks and am sorry I could not include all of their wonderful stories.

Thank you to Bill Bishop, president of Bishop Information Group, who turned my first ideas into a reality over ten years ago. Thank you to Dan Sullivan and his Strategic Coach program for entrepreneurs, which gave me the support and inspiration to follow the dreams I imagined for myself and my family.

Thank you as well to Justin Nichols, who drew the cartoons for the original version of the book. His playful approach to the subject of money kept me on track.

Thanks to my business associates who provided helpful feedback and honest criticism in regards to this project. I would especially like to thank my terrific business partner, Sherry, and her husband, Fred, whose wisdom, friendship, and support have been invaluable. Also Kelly, Mike, and Cathy, who added their own unique perspectives to my work.

And very importantly, I want to thank my parents, Dick and Norma, and my sisters, Carol, Dianne, and Christine, and their families, who influenced my entrepreneurial choices and motivated me to excel. Their love and support continues to be an important foundation in my life.

Thank you to our sons, Ryan, Patrick, and Jeremy, who are such a blessing to me. They continue to teach me about making allowances and in their own ways have become entrepreneurs themselves. I look forward to the lessons they will teach me in the future.

Finally, I wish to thank my Lord Jesus Christ, who offers hope, forgiveness, and love every day.

Train a child in the way that he should go,
and when he is old he will not turn from it.
—Proverbs 22:6

Worksheets

Introduction

Kids and Money: Building a Solid Foundation

As a certified financial planner, I thought I would have no trouble coaching my kids to handle money responsibly. But when I decided to give my three sons an allowance to buy candy, toys, running shoes, and a million other things, I was just like every other parent. I did not know where to start or what steps to take. And because I counseled adults on managing their finances, my lack of expertise when it came to coaching my own kids really surprised me.

At that point my wife and I set out to learn how to teach our kids to handle money. We have used a variety of techniques, and our boys have developed confident money-management skills. Over the years, I have developed and refined a complete program to teach kids about money. I call this the Making Allowances System. My wife and I have been extremely pleased with the results, and this system has also worked for our friends, relatives, and associates. This book aims to help other parents have similar success.

Addressing a social problem

In the work I do, I have observed that many adults do not know how to handle money responsibly. My hunch is that this is because they did not handle money enough when they were children.

Their parents did all of the spending, banking, and saving. They may have received an allowance, but it was used only to make small purchases. Unfortunately, they may never have learned how to save money for more expensive items or for long-term investments. It is no wonder many adults in our society are hooked on credit cards and live month to month, spending all of their incomes. They never learned basic money skills as children.

If you want your children to grow up to be financially responsible adults, I believe you must let them handle money often. At an early age, they need to handle money and understand the importance of depositing money in a bank on a regular basis. They also need to develop the habit of saving money for major purchases. These lessons will help your children develop a much more comprehensive understanding of money and how to manage it.

Giving an allowance sets the groundwork for good money management because it provides an opportunity for parents to help their children develop good habits that will stay with them for life. If you can teach your children to save, spend, and invest responsibly, you will prepare them for a productive, successful life.

This book shares the insights I have gained from my personal experience of teaching kids about money. But before we get into the details of the Making Allowances System, let us have a quick look at the dangers and opportunities you face as a parent in regard to your kids and money.

Kids and Money: The Dangers

Perhaps you are one of many adults who did not learn good money management from your own parents. Yet at some point in your life you managed to pick up the information and skills you needed. Maybe you think your kids will manage just as well. I am not out to scare you, but as a parent, you face six key dangers if you do not have a system for teaching your kids healthy habits and attitudes about money.

Financial dependency

If you do not teach your children properly about money, they could grow up with poor money handling skills and become financially irresponsible adults. They might end up spending every cent they earn, living paycheck to paycheck. They could become mired in debt or, even worse, they could remain financially dependent on you when you should be saving for, or enjoying, your retirement. In fact, how you teach your kids about money now could affect your own personal wealth in the future.

Destructive values

Because they lack positive money-management habits and attitudes, your children could adopt destructive values about money. In today's complex, consumer-oriented, media-saturated world, your kids might adopt values about money that completely contradict your own. For example, they might come to equate money with self-worth. They might become hooked on acquiring possessions, on keeping up with the crowd, on always staying in fashion. They might adopt the attitude that you are always available to bail them out when they need money, that if they want something, all they need to do is ask for it. They might develop unrealistic expectations, believing they are entitled to all the latest gadgets, even believing their happiness depends on having them.

The debt trap

If you do not teach your kids about money when they are young, they could grow up to be victims of our credit and consumer culture. They might develop poor money-management habits as adults and possibly end up in paralyzing debt. Consider that they could enter their twenties and thirties not knowing how to set financial goals, how to save money for the future, how to make a budget, how to plan buying decisions, and how to be smart consumers. Newspapers often carry stories of young adults on the brink of financial disaster.

Loss of confidence

Without positive money habits and good life skills, your children could become adults lacking confidence to make the right financial decisions. This lack of financial confidence could affect your children's confidence in other areas of their lives.

Negative lessons

Although you want to take an active role in teaching your kids about money, without proper guidance, you could unintentionally go astray. For example, you might use money to motivate your kids to score goals or earn better marks. These bribes, discussed in chapter 2, can teach your kids to equate money with success, to believe that money is the only real reward for an achievement. In this way, you might teach your kids the wrong values even when you have all the best intentions. To avoid such a result, this book stresses the importance of "principles." You and your children need to think about your money principles before you take action. By observing the principles, you will be less likely to take missteps.

Family conflict

If you do not make a concerted effort to teach your children good money skills and attitudes, you could make a negative impact on your family relationships because of conflicts related to money. In my opinion, this danger is the most serious. It is not uncommon for families to be torn apart by disputes over business and inheritances. Even when the sums are modest, money-related tensions can arise. This tension between spouses and between parents and their children can destroy the love and joy that should be a part of marriage and family life. If you lack strong money principles and a plan of action, your relationship with your kids could be consumed with arguments over allowance(s) and other financial issues. Believe me, I have seen this happen all too often.

Since I started developing the Making Allowances System, I have noticed that most parents feel threatened by these dangers—either because they did nothing to teach their kids about money or because they thought their own good financial habits would somehow rub off on their kids. For the most part, we parents lack the knowledge, structure, and tools to teach our kids helpful money-management skills. This book was written to provide you with this know-how and thus help you and your children avoid these potential dangers.

Kids, Parents, and Money: The Benefits

On the plus side of the ledger, this book will help you take advantage of the many positive results when you teach your kids about money. The benefits for you and your family are legion, but six major ones stand out: financial responsibility, strong positive values about money, useful money-management skills, increased self-confidence (for both you and your kids), and better relationships.

Financial responsibility as adults

If you help your kids develop good money habits when they are young, they will have a better chance of being successful as adults. They will learn to make choices, will become more independent, and will know how to set and achieve financial goals.

Strong positive values about money

You have an opportunity to help your kids develop a good attitude toward money; you can teach them that money is not an end in itself, but a means to achieve more important goals in their lives. They can develop a sense of self-worth that is not tied to the size of their bank accounts or to the kind of running shoes they wear. Also, if they develop a good attitude toward money, they may be better able to resist the negative aspects of peer pressure.

Consistent money habits and useful financial skills

With your help, your kids can grow up knowing how to set financial goals, how to follow a budget, and how to handle money on a daily basis. They will also learn to save money regularly, make smart buying decisions, and set their own priorities on spending.

Confidence to make their own choices

By teaching your kids how to handle their own money from an early age, you will give them increasing confidence to make their own choices. They will not feel they always need to turn to you and other people to make decisions for them. If they develop confidence about money early on, they will be better able to handle increasing responsibility as they get older. Also, their confidence about money will translate into confidence about other areas of their lives, such as school, athletics, personal relationships, and community involvement.

Confidence that you are doing the right thing

If you follow the proven process set out in this book, you will become more confident about teaching your kids. You will see results throughout their childhood and teen years. You will know you are teaching the right principles the right way, which will boost your own self-esteem as a parent. (That is not to say you will agree with everything I say in this book, but it will help you decide what is right for you, and that will further increase your confidence.)

Improved relationships with your kids

As you work with your kids on the concepts around money, you have the opportunity to discuss thousands of topics. That is because money issues affect virtually every area of our lives. As you progress, you will learn a lot about your kids, and they will learn a lot about you. You will also work as a team, instead of as adversaries. This chance to be a team is, in my mind, the greatest opportunity of all.

The Making Allowances System

Helping you avoid these dangers and realize these opportunities and benefits is the purpose behind the Making Allowances System. It provides the principles, structure, and tools you need to teach your kids about money. The system is presented step-by-step as a series of distinct concepts (one per chapter) to help support you in your knowledge of money management. Each concept contains the following primary components:

Achievable goals

At the start of each chapter, you will see three goals listed—what the chapter aims to teach both you and your children. All of the principles, structures, and tools presented in each chapter are designed to help you achieve these goals.

Helpful guidelines

Each chapter presents key guidelines for how best to teach your kids each concept. Following these guidelines will give you more confidence when you are teaching your kids. It will also make it easier for your kids to understand why you want them to do things a certain way. Build upon what you are doing well and what you see will be best for each of your children.

A step-by-step system

Lack of structure is one major weakness of most books about kids and money. They contain a lot of useful information, but they do not give you any real ideas about how to put this information into action. The Making Allowances System is different. Each chapter focuses on a specific concept and concludes with a step-by-step summary. This structure will bolster your confidence, and it will also help your kids learn faster and more effectively. The first six chapters are best completed in order, as the concepts build upon one another; later chapters can be addressed as slowly or quickly as your family decides.

Worksheets, Tips & Traps, and Reality Checks

To help you teach your kids important money concepts, and to keep everyone on track, the book includes practical tools such as worksheets for your family to work on together (also available via my website, www.paullermitte.com). The worksheets are not mandatory but can be helpful to reinforce the discussions you are having with your kids, especially if more structure is needed. There are plenty of take-action tips and cautionary notes in the "Tips & Traps" sidebars. In addition, I share kids-and-money stories from my own life and from the experiences of other people in the boxes titled "Reality Check."

In an attempt to be gender neutral, the text alternates between the use of "he" and "she," "his" and "her." However, I make no effort to use feminine and masculine pronouns in precisely equal numbers. In the words of the personal finances author Jean Ross Peterson, "Any child is every child, and it is children who are important." Families also come in all shapes and sizes. Not all of

Making inexpensive mistakes when you are a child and learning from them is far better than making costly mistakes as an adult.

them have two parents or more than one child; children may be from blended families, diverse cultures, or raised by their grand-parents. I aim to be inclusive but tend to refer to the traditional family model most often, simply because that is the one I am most familiar with. Please forgive this bias and adapt the advice for your own situation.

So What About You?

Here is one thing I have learned about parents: they can often be very hard on themselves. They worry that they are not doing the right things, that they are not spending enough time with their kids, that they are too strict or too lax. No matter what they do, they do not think it is enough. Well, if you are in this camp, I am here to tell you that things are not as bad as they seem. If you have kids of school age, you owe yourself a pat on the back.

You have managed the following:

- You have children. This is a major achievement in itself, because you have accepted the responsibility of being a parent and you have made a huge commitment.

- You love your kids. You would not be reading this book if you didn't. You provide a caring, nurturing environment for your kids.

- You have helped your children develop some important skills and habits.

- You have probably started some kind of money program with your kids (allowance, regular savings, bank accounts), and you have established some policies about chores and treats.

- You have worked on your own personal financial habits. You may have a regular savings plan, an education savings plan, an investment portfolio, and other cornerstones of sound financial planning (for example, wills and insurance).

So there you go. Things are a lot better than you might think. All of these accomplishments are the stepping stones to your next stage as a parent: beginning to teach your kids about the world of money. You are ready to begin using the Making Allowances System.

A Little About Me

So why am I qualified to write this book? Well, first of all, I am a parent myself. I have been using this system with my three boys—Ryan, Patrick, and Jeremy—for more than twenty years. I have proven it works with my kids (who have become financially mature young adults) and with many other parents and their kids.

In addition to my qualifications as a parent, I am also a certified financial planner with more than twenty-five years of experience. Working with hundreds of individuals and couples, most of whom are parents, I have learned firsthand the problems and challenges parents face when teaching their kids about money.

But most of all, I am qualified to help you teach your kids because I am passionate about helping parents and their kids learn money-management skills. I have developed and tested every principle in this book because I believe that everyone can benefit from these skills. The system works, and I want to share with you the same good experience I have had with my kids.

The Universal Principles

As mentioned, in each chapter I provide several key principles to help you teach and implement each concept. These subprinciples are based on a number of universal principles that you should understand right from the start. These principles are as follows:

Talk about it

Maintaining an ongoing dialogue with your kids is the best way to teach them about money. Whenever you introduce a new concept or face a showdown over a money-related issue, the most effective way to address it is to talk about it. Choosing an appropriate time to talk is also important.

Start early

Ideally, start working with your children at an early age, preferably age five or six. If you wait until your kids are in their teens, it will be more difficult (but not impossible) to teach them new money principles and concepts. Stick to the system presented in this book to bring your teens to the skill level they need.

Give up control

To learn about money, your kids have to do things themselves. Instead of handling their money for them, let them do it. Let them make deposits and withdrawals from the bank; let them make their own purchases; let them decide what they want to buy with their own money. You can offer advice, but let them do it on their own. Hands-on practice is the best way to learn any new skill.

Let your kids make mistakes

Even if you think your kids are spending their allowance on the wrong things, let them do it. Do not intervene and take charge. Let them make mistakes. If they mess up, they will learn the lesson much faster than by listening to a lecture. After all, making inexpensive mistakes when you are a child and learning from them is far better than making costly mistakes as an adult.

Set limits

Although you need to give your kids money for allowance, for treats on special occasions, and for the purchase of trendy clothes and other stuff, you also have to set limits. You must teach your kids that money does not come pouring out of bank machines. They have to learn to make choices based on financial limits. Even if you have a large income and oodles of money to spend on your kids, they will learn to manage money well only if they operate within some kind of set budget. So set limits.

Provide structure

Your job as a parent is to help your kids express their individuality and creativity within a well-defined structure. This is especially important when you teach your kids about money. You need to help them establish a consistent regime of allowance, saving, and spending. This type of structure will help them learn faster and with more confidence.

How to Make Allowances

As you work through the Making Allowances System with your kids, keep a sense of humor. When the unexpected happens—and it will—go with the flow. Improvise. Let your kids make mistakes. Let yourself make mistakes. Make allowances. Most of all, enjoy your relationship with your children.

As you read, take note of the ideas that particularly grab you. What ideas make sense to you and seem reasonable to try in your family? You may want to implement the concepts slowly and limit yourself to one concept per month. Or perhaps you have teenagers and feel the need to jump in and implement many concepts at once. Whatever your situation, there is help to be had.

You may find that some of the concepts will not work well for you or may not apply to your particular situation. The important thing is for you and your children to talk about money and learn how to manage it—both independently and together. I hope you and your children enjoy this book. I am excited about the adventure ahead of you and wish you well as you begin to "make allowances." I invite your feedback, advice, and personal stories on my website, www.paullermitte.com. You can also e-mail me at paul@paullermitte.com.

1

The Allowance Contract

Teaching your children

- the value of money

- the basics of good money management

- to begin a lifelong habit of saving

WHEN YOUR CHILD reaches the age of five or six, it is time to introduce her to the world of money. By this age, she will be familiar with money on several levels—she can count it, identify the different denominations, and recognize that she needs a specific amount to buy the goods she wants. Thus, it is a natural time to start giving your child an allowance, to establish an "allowance system."

Some children may be ready at a younger age, especially if they are avid counters or shoppers. But I would urge you not to rush your children. Preschoolers can be given change to put in their piggy bank or to purchase a candy bar, but an allowance is not necessary.

Establishing an allowance system may sound like a simple matter, but it may not always be straightforward. Here are some questions you might ask yourself:

- Should I give my child an allowance at all?

- If so, how much money should I give?

- When should I give it?

- What should the allowance be used for?

- If I give my child an allowance, who pays for special treats?

- Should my child earn the allowance by doing chores around the house?

- Should the allowance be tied to achievement at school or used to encourage good behavior?

- Should part of the money be put in the bank as savings?

- Should I transfer funds automatically from my account to my child's?

In most cases, parents answer their questions about allowance by drawing on their own experiences. They say: "When I was her age, I got 25 cents a week for allowance, and it was plenty." Or they say: "I didn't get any allowance. I had to earn money by doing chores around the house." Parents also consider examples set by relatives, friends, and neighbors. They say: "His cousin gets an allowance of $20 a month, so that's what we'll do." Or they say: "Suzie across the street only gets an allowance if she makes her bed every day."

Unfortunately, taking your lead from the past, or from people around you, is a risky strategy. What worked twenty-five years ago may not work today. The world, and kids, have changed dramatically since you were growing up. Today we are bombarded with more advertising and much more product choice. Many of us lead busier, more stressful lives than our parents did. In the same way, what appears to work across the street might be the wrong approach in your house. Every family has different values, customs, income levels, and attitudes toward money.

"Chores begin when your child can pick it up, put it away, fold it, sort it, or carry it out the door."

Jean Ross Peterson, author on financial issues

So what can you do when faced with all these divergent examples? The solution is quite simple, really. Create your approach based on certain principles that have been proven to work over and over again, by my own family and by the families of many of my clients and friends. I call these "The Key Allowance Guidelines." In setting them out and providing the Allowance Contract, I aim to help you

- introduce your children to the value of money

- teach them the basics of good money management

- establish in your children a lifelong habit of saving

The Key Allowance Guidelines

In this chapter I'd like to state these guidelines twice because they really set the foundation for much of the financial advice to come. The five key allowance guidelines are as follows:

1. Make a promise to your child

2. Have your child make a promise to you

3. Be consistent and firm

4. Do not tie allowance to chores or achievement

5. Make savings part of the allowance contract

Let's look at each of these guidelines in more detail.

1. Make a promise to your child

You may choose to give the first allowance as a significant rite of passage. You could tell your children: "When you turn five [or six … or whatever age you decide], you will start getting an allowance." This approach is helpful in families with several children because young children have something to look forward to. Explain to your children that an allowance is a set amount of money, given weekly, to enable them to pay for things that are important to them, such as toys, candy, video games, or books.

Before you start your allowance system, promise your child a specific amount of money on a specific day of every week. Give an amount you deem appropriate. My guideline is one dollar times half their age, per week. (I discuss this suggestion in greater detail later in the chapter.) Establish a day of the week, such as Sunday or Monday, that makes sense for your family situation. Of course, the point of making the promise is that you keep it.

2. Have your child make a promise to you

Before she receives the allowance, suggest that your child promise you two things. One, she will set aside part of the allowance for savings. Two, the rest of her money will be "mad money"—used for fun—and she will not ask you for more when it is all gone. If she does not have enough money to buy everything she wants, she can do extra odd jobs around the house for payment or find small jobs to do around the neighborhood.

3. Be consistent and firm

Once you start giving your child an allowance, try to be consistent, and give the amount of money you promised, on the day you promised. Remember, your child looks forward to that allowance the same way you anticipate your paycheck. If your child spends his allowance right away, do not top it up! Tell your child he will have to wait until the next allowance day. You may hear some whining and even slamming of doors once in a while, but this will not go on year after year. If you hold firm, your child will know the buck stops there. If your child thinks you will always give more money if his runs out, he will never learn to *manage* the allowance.

4. Do not tie allowance to chores or achievement

A child should receive an allowance for being part of a family. The majority of financial psychologists and counselors agree that an allowance should not be tied to personal achievements, such as getting an A on a report card or winning a softball championship. (See chapter 2 for more discussion of this issue.) Encourage hard work and good behavior, and reward achievement in other meaningful ways. In other words, do not use an allowance as a bribe or a reward. Give an allowance to teach your children the basics of good money management.

5. Make savings part of the allowance contract

Saving money is a habit that should be learned at an early age. The best time to begin teaching this habit is the first time you give your child an allowance. I suggest you require your child to save 25 percent of his allowance each week and put the savings in the bank, or a piggy bank, every month. Help him set a goal for something he would like to buy with the savings. Ask him to agree to keep the savings for the first three months, to build patience and a larger savings amount.

In my experience as both a parent and a professional financial planner advising families in business, these five allowance guidelines are very important. When our children were growing up, each had their own money to spend on treats. They purchased toys and books with their own savings, accumulated spending money for family holidays, gave money to charity, and put long-term savings into mutual funds. We used these same allowance guidelines to teach our children good money-management skills. If you incorporate these guidelines into your routines, your children will learn valuable lessons about money and develop skills and habits that will last a lifetime.

Setting Up an Allowance System

To help you implement the five allowance guidelines, I created the Allowance Contract, which you can use to set up your own allowance system with your child. The contract walks you through a step-by-step system that has worked in my family and in thousands of others.

After reading chapters 1, 2, and 3, sit down with your younger children and review the Allowance Contract (see Worksheet 1.1). Explain to them that a contract is a promise or agreement to do something. Give them an opportunity to ask questions, and bring up questions if your children do not. The important thing is to get them thinking about money and how to handle it.

For older children age twelve and up, also read chapter 4, and then share the concepts with them. You may even want to read parts of the chapters together. Do not skip steps. Remember, these are habit-forming life skills that will impact your children for a lifetime. Your goal in giving an allowance is to create money-smart kids who are able to spend wisely, save for the future, and make good consumer decisions at all stages of life.

Here are some key considerations when setting up your allowance system.

The amount and the day

First, determine the amount of the allowance and the day of the week for giving it. Give careful consideration to choosing an amount. One guideline would be to give an amount equal to half the age of the child (e.g., a 10-year-old would receive $5 a week). Another option is to give a dollar amount per the age of the child (e.g., $10 a week for a 10-year-old).

An amount equal to half the age of the child works well for most families. This amount gives the child some spending money and leaves enough to save to make average purchases over a month or two.

Also, such an amount is not so much that your children can buy whatever they want. They are still motivated to do odd jobs or look for ways to earn money, especially as they get older and their interests and hobbies often become more expensive. Cash and gift cards are often given as gifts these days, so the child usually has another source of savings that can be added to the allowance.

Realistically, the amount you decide on will depend on your financial situation. Decide on an amount that you know you can pay out every week and which will also give your child a reasonable amount of savings and weekly spending money.

Give the allowance in coins, especially to young children. This will help them to understand better the amount of money they are receiving (and gives them practical math skills, too). In addition, coins can easily be divided into amounts for the piggy bank and the wallet. Handling money each week will build good, practical habits for the future.

I also recommend you give the allowance on Sunday night or on Monday. If you give it on Friday, all of it may tend to disappear over the weekend.

Savings for the future

Figure out how much you want your child to save. I recommend 25 percent, but you can set this figure as more or less. Financial experts often suggest that adults set aside a minimum of 10 percent of their income for savings. If we can start our kids with a higher ideal, when they are older they will see 10 percent as an easy goal to attain. Teaching children to save will help them to become good financial managers and become financially independent. This, in turn, will help you, the parent, put away your long-term savings because you will not have to fund the lifestyle of your young adult!

Do not relent when your child comes to you midweek asking for more money, above and beyond their allowance.

Sometimes the child wants to try to save more than 25 percent, but saving too much money can pose a problem. If the remaining money is not adequate to cover those trips to the corner store, your child will be tempted to raid their piggy bank and upset the savings plan, or come to you for more money.

Get a piggy bank and wallet

Go out with your child and buy a wallet and the kind of piggy bank you can open without breaking. For young children age four and up, it is especially important to handle the money. The piggy bank is for their savings, and the wallet is for their spending money. Having both gives the child a concrete understanding of the two concepts: saving and spending. If you have children over age ten, a bank account can take the place of the piggy bank.

As soon as you give the allowance to your child, have her put the savings portion into the piggy bank. At the end of the month, you can go to the bank with your child, set up an account, and deposit the accumulated savings. As agreed, the savings will not be withdrawn for three months, to allow a large amount to build. After the three-month startup period, the savings can be withdrawn at any time to purchase the items listed in the contract. (Using this saving method is good training to prevent impulse buying.)

Hold firm to your agreement

It may be hard, but do not relent when your child comes to you midweek asking for more money, above and beyond their allowance. Your child has to learn that money does not come free from the bank machine, in endless amounts. Be consistent. Stick to your part of the Allowance Contract and expect your children to do the same.

The Allowance Contract

Creating the Allowance Contract is the next step in establishing a consistent allowance system. Before you give your child the allowance, sit down together and work out a simple contract. In the contract, you promise to give a set amount of allowance on a given day of the week. In return, your child promises to:

- save 25 percent of the allowance

- put the savings in the bank at the end of the month

- not withdraw savings from the bank for the first three months

- spend the savings on items related to their personal goals

Committing to these promises teaches your child about developing good financial habits, setting goals, and making a commitment. Working through the Allowance Contract is a lot of fun

Our Allowance Contract

(Child) I, _____ , will:

- receive $ _____ allowance every Sunday/Monday

- put _____ % of allowance away for savings

- visit the bank on the last Saturday of every month to deposit savings

- retrieve savings only after they reach a minimum of $ _____

- supply an outline of what allowance and savings will be used for

(Parent) I, _____ , will:

- pay $ _____ allowance every Sunday/Monday

- receive an outline of what allowance will be used for _____

- receive an outline of what savings will be used for: short and long term

I, _____ , will use my allowance for the following:

-

-

-

-

I, _____ , will use my savings for the following:

-

-

-

-

_____   _____
Child   Parent

_____   _____
Date   Date

Worksheet 1.1

(kids generally love "making a deal"). Also, the process gives your child the opportunity to ask questions about money. You will be surprised at the questions children ask!

Use the ready-made Allowance Contract on page 37, download a copy free from www.paullermitte.com, or put together your own contract.

The Allowance Tracker is a visual reminder that the allowance has been paid.

The Allowance Tracker

To help you be consistent in giving allowance, I suggest you keep a written record of the allowance you have given out. You can do this in a notebook or use the Allowance Tracker form opposite. This has been one of the most important forms for our family, because it is a visual reminder that the allowance has been paid.

Let's say that your usual night to give out allowance is Monday, and you realize at 9:00 PM that not only have you forgotten to pay, but you do not have the correct change in your wallet. It is late, it is raining, and you decide to pay the allowance on Tuesday instead. Then, before you know it, Friday arrives, and you cannot remember if you paid the allowance this week or not.

Allowance Tracker

Date	CHILD 1	CHILD 2	CHILD 3
MONTH			
Week 1			
Week 2			
Week 3			
Week 4			
Week 5			
Other Job(s)			
MONTH			
Week 1			
Week 2			
Week 3			
Week 4			
Week 5			
Other Job(s)			
MONTH			
Week 1			
Week 2			
Week 3			
Week 4			
Week 5			
Other Job(s)			

Worksheet 1.2

Keeping a record enables you to figure out when you last paid out allowance, and how much. In addition, when your child complains that he has not received his allowance "for at least three weeks!" you can pull out your record and the discussion is over. You will either have to apologize and pay out—or you can smile smugly.

This tracking method is especially helpful if there are multiple children in your family or if you have a shared parenting arrangement. Another great idea, suggested by a colleague, is to prepare allowance envelopes with the correct change at the beginning of each month, to avoid not having the correct amount on hand.

Step-by-Step Summary

1. **Decide on the specific amount for the allowance.**

   I have suggested one dollar times half your child's age, per week. So, for example, a five-year-old would receive $2.50. An alternative is to double that amount, giving a dollar amount that matches each child's age (e.g., $10 per week for a 10-year-old). This allows some spending money as well as the opportunity to save for larger purchases. Each family is different, and you should set the amount that fits yours.

2. **Decide the day of the week to give the allowance.**

   I recommend giving an allowance on Sunday night or on Monday. If a child receives their allowance on Friday, they may be tempted to spend it all over the weekend.

3. **Decide on the savings amount.**

   Financial experts recommend a saving rate of 10 percent for adults. The idea here is to start our kids with an even higher ideal of 25 percent, so they will establish the habit of saving and become financially independent.

4. **Talk to your child and explain the Allowance Contract.**

   Discussing the contract gives your child the opportunity to ask questions about money. The contract by its very nature is mutual, with both parent and child having input—and a stake in the allowance system.

5. **Prepare the contract together and sign it.**

   Use the Allowance Contract provided or feel free to create your own. Having a written contract makes the process more formal and important, to both you and your children.

6. **Give the allowance on a predetermined day (in coins).**

   Coins are recommended, especially for young children, to help them understand the amount of money they are receiving. Also, coins can be easily divided between piggy bank (savings) and wallet (spending money).

7. **Have your child put savings in their piggy bank.**

   Some children may wish to save more than 25 percent, but this can cause problems if the remaining allowance does not cover treats during the week.

8. **Have your child put the rest of the allowance in their wallet.**

   The reason for having both a piggy bank and a wallet is to give your children a concrete understanding of both saving and spending.

9. *At the end of the month, put the accumulated savings into the bank.*

    Make the trip to the bank with your children, so they can see where their savings are going and learn about banking from a young age.

10. *Track your payment of allowance using a notebook or the Allowance Tracker form.*

    When memory fails or questions arise, you will have a written record of when you last paid allowance and how much.

2

Tricks or Treats?

Teaching your children

- about generosity, sharing, and appreciation

Strategies for parents

- differentiate between allowance, treats, and family expenditures

- give treats without negatively affecting good allowance habits

WHEN YOU AND YOUR CHILDREN have established a regular allowance system, it is time to face the next major issue related to kids and money: treats.

If you give your children $5 or $10 in allowance every Sunday night, you might ask yourself: "Why should I treat my kids to special snacks or outings if I already give them money every week?" Or "Why should I reward my children for their good report cards if I give them an allowance?" And what about regular outings to movies, football games, or concerts? Are these considered treats or something else? Should kids be required to pay for their own entertainment tickets out of their allowance? These are all great questions that this chapter aims to address.

Allowance, Treats, or Family Expenditures?

The difference between these three concepts—allowance, treats, and regular family expenditures—can get blurred, especially in your child's mind. And this confusion can undermine the good habits you are trying to instill with the Allowance Contract. So it is important to make the distinctions between the concepts as clear as possible. Here is one way to think about the difference, so you can explain it to your children.

Allowance

An allowance is given to a child on a regular, consistent basis. In simple terms, a child should receive his allowance for simply being a member of the family, in order to learn good money-management skills. It is used by the child to buy items for himself or for others.

Allowance is not given as a treat or as a reward, nor is it taken away as a punishment. The money should not be used to pay for family outings, unless these outings are the idea of the child—a movie, for example. In our family, when the kids asked to go out for a fast-food lunch, we offered to drive, if they paid for their own lunch.

Money is a commodity of exchange and is not an exchange of value or worth.

Treats

Treats are given by parents to model positive values, such as generosity, sharing, togetherness, fun, and appreciation. Treats can be given spontaneously, such as when you have been at a baseball practice and decide to pull into a convenience store to buy everyone a cold drink.

Treats can also be planned. For example, you might take a child on a monthly "date." Or perhaps you have a tradition of taking the kids out for breakfast on the first day of school. Finally, treats can be given as a reward for the achievement of a goal. You might take your honor-roll student out for a special lunch or buy your swimmer a new bathing suit when he beats his personal best.

We had a reluctant reader at our house and found that if we rewarded him with a new book when he finished reading one, he became excited about reading. Today he is a voracious reader, and the added bonus at the time was that his school grades improved.

Most counselors and child specialists believe it is better to give a reward with something tangible than to give money. Money is a commodity of exchange and is not an exchange of value or worth. Do not let your child equate her self-esteem and worth with the amount of money she receives.

Family expenditures

Family expenditures are made on a regular basis and are paid for by the parents. For example, the family might buy pizza on Friday nights or go bowling every Saturday afternoon. The child is not required to contribute part of his allowance. Like allowance, these expenditures are given for simply being a member of the family.

REALITY CHECK

When our family went on long road trips, we provided the meals and the children paid for their own treats. Decide what guidelines will work for your family, discuss them with your children, and then stick with them.

Five Key Treats Guidelines

Here are five key pointers to guide you through the minefield of family spending as it relates to your children.

1. Distinguish between allowance and treats

Communicate clearly to your child when you expect her to use her allowance and when you will be paying for treats. Review the Allowance Contract with your child and go over again what she can buy with her allowance. Talk about other things you might buy as a treat. Create a list of treats with your child and then discuss reasons why you would give her one:

- as a reward: for bringing home a good report card, passing a grade, achieving a goal, demonstrating good behavior, and being helpful; or

- spontaneously: on the spur of the moment to express affection, appreciation, and generosity

Decide and agree as parents whether treats should include larger items such as clothes or only small, inexpensive items.

2. Make the distinction between treats and family expenditures

Speak to your child about the difference between a treat (given spontaneously or as a planned reward) and a regular family expenditure, such as a weekly chocolate bar or trips to the zoo. Create a list of such items. Explain that she does not need to contribute to these family expenditures.

3. Give treats to model positive values

When treats are given as a reward, they teach your child such values as hard work, achievement, and appreciation. When treats are given spontaneously, they teach your child about generosity, sharing, and togetherness. Treats also teach your kids how to say "please" and "thank you," and provide a model for the important principle of "sharing the wealth" when we have an abundance of good fortune.

4. Give treats to encourage positive lifestyle choices

Treats do not have to come in the form of candy, fast food, or a trip to the arcade. While your child may ask you for these things, you can choose other treats that you consider more positive, such as educational toys, books, or tickets to a concert, play, or sporting event.

5. Do not try to create the perfect balance among siblings

If you have two or more children, doling out treats can cause a serious outbreak of sibling rivalry. When one child is given a treat, the other child may feel he is falling behind in the great "treat" register in the sky. If this happens, do not try to level the playing field. Children have to learn that life is not about making sure everything comes out evenly. Sometimes there is an imbalance, but that is the way it goes. This is normal!

Do not get upset when your kids cry or yell or express anger toward you. Help them understand. If you give in and try to even the score, your children will begin to view treats as a "right" rather than something that is given or received as a privilege.

The problem of sibling rivalry can be especially difficult when you have children with large gaps between ages. For example, you might give your 16-year-old a $100 track suit and your 9-year-old a $20 T-shirt. There is a vast difference in the money spent, but your 9-year-old should not expect you to spend $100 on him as well. So again, don't try to even the score. Give treats when and how you see fit. But be consistent so as not to play favorites. And no matter what your family looks like, it helps for parents to communicate with one another to keep a balance.

When our family went out to the movies as a family event, we parents made a family expenditure. If one of the children wished to go with a friend to a movie, he used some of his own allowance. Younger children could pay a portion and teens pay for the ticket on their own—especially if they are working.

The Treats Planner

Giving treats to your children can be one of the greatest pleasures in life. It is satisfying to see them break into a wide grin when you give them a treat. The trick, as I have said, is to keep treats separate from allowance and family expenditures. It is also important not to spoil your kids. Otherwise, they will come to expect treats on a regular basis and will not appreciate them.

You may wish to use a Treats Planner worksheet like that on the next page to keep track of all of the treats you give to your kids: what you bought, where you bought it, and how much you spent. You should also keep track of why you gave them the treat and their reaction to it.

This record can be used to see your patterns of giving treats or to solve a problem. For example, perhaps one of your children is more demanding or insistent than the others and seems to get more than her fair share of treats. You can use your treats planner to monitor the situation. You may decide it is best not to share this information with your children.

A treats planner is not meant to take the fun and spontaneity out of giving treats. It is designed to help you and your kids keep track of what you are doing and to identify ways to improve the

Treats Planner for Parents

Treat			
Where		Reason	
Cost		Response	
Treat			
Where		Reason	
Cost		Response	
Treat			
Where		Reason	
Cost		Response	
Treat			
Where		Reason	
Cost		Response	
Treat			
Where		Reason	
Cost		Response	
Treat			
Where		Reason	
Cost		Response	
Treat			
Where		Reason	
Cost		Response	
Treat			
Where		Reason	
Cost		Response	

Worksheet 2.1

process. In fact, it is only meant to be used for a brief time. Once you and your children have developed your own way of handling treats, you will no longer need the form.

REALITY CHECK

I had the boys help do a spring cleanup of the deck. It was a time-consuming, tiresome job that the kids grumbled through. After they completed the job, I took them to a favorite ice cream store as a reward for sticking with it. However, I had made no mention of the possibility of a treat beforehand.

Treats Tips & Traps

1. **No thanks for treats:** If your child does not appreciate a treat, do not scold him or vow to cut out treats altogether. At a later time, speak to your child about what happened. Express your disappointment in his behavior. Explain that a treat is to be appreciated, and you wish to receive a polite expression of gratitude when you give a treat.

2. **Do not give money as a reward:** Instead of money, give something more meaningful to reward an achievement, such as an educational toy, book, or trip to a sports or cultural event.

3. **Let kids decide:** If you want to motivate your children, let them decide on the treats they want as a reward. Of course, you can help with ideas and set a reasonable budget, but from my experience, children get more excited about a treat they themselves have chosen, rather than one decided on by a parent.

4. **How to handle birthdays and special holidays:** Special days such as birthdays and other seasonal or cultural events

can turn into an avalanche of gift giving. At a time when your kids are getting lots of presents and special treats from their relatives, it is important for you to make a clear distinction about a special treat. If you are going to give an additional treat over a holiday, communicate as clearly as possible the reason that you are providing the treat. Note: I find it is during these special occasions that I worry the most about spoiling children. It is helpful to have a budgeted amount to keep within the boundaries of our own cash management.

5. **Handling generous relatives:** Your children may have relatives who love to lavish treats and presents on them. Although on one hand this generosity is wonderful, on the other hand it can raise the expectations of your children much higher than you want. If this happens, I suggest you talk to the relatives about the issue and see if they can bring their generosity more in line with your own. If they continue to give an excess of treats, you will need to speak with your children and explain that the relatives' style of giving treats is different from your own.

Step-by-Step Summary

1. ***Consider the difference between allowance, treats, and family expenditures.***

    Whether they live together or apart, it will be best if both parents have a clear understanding of the difference between these three concepts, so they can be consistent with expenditures and present a "united front" to the children.

2. ***Decide what to include in each of these categories.***

    Allowance is not a treat or reward and, as a rule, this money is not used to pay for family outings. Treats can be given spontaneously or as a planned reward. Family expen-

ditures, paid for by the parents, cover regular events such as weekly family outings or activities.

3. **Decide when treats will be given, when allowances will be paid, and which costs will be considered family expenditures.**

   Treats can be given to model positive values, encourage positive lifestyle choices, and reward success. Keeping a treats planner can help you keep track of treats. The important thing is to distinguish them from allowance and family expenditures.

4. **Go over the Allowance Contract with your children.**

   Discuss what treats they will buy for themselves and how much money they are to save. You can use this opportunity to discuss the kinds of things you might give to your children as treats, separate from allowance—and your reasons for giving them.

5. **Discuss with your children some ideas for treats and family expenditures.**

   Creating a list of both treats and family expenditures can be helpful to clarify the distinction between these two categories. And allowing kids to decide on their own rewards can be a great motivator.

6. **Discuss with your children how treats may differ between them, based on age and interests.**

   It only makes sense that a 5-year-old will have different interests and hobbies than a 15-year-old—with different costs attached. If you explain it diplomatically, children should be able to understand this concept and know that "all's fair" in the family. Aim for fairness, of course, but do not feel you have to "even the score" between siblings.

3

Laughing All the Way to the Bank

Teaching your children

- how to save money regularly

- about banks and how they work

- how to deal with people with regard to money matters

MANY ADULTS do not know how to handle money properly because they did not handle money enough when they were children. Instead, their parents did all of the spending, banking, and saving. If you want your children to grow up to be financially responsible adults, you need to let them handle money often.

At an early age, children should learn how banks work and why it is important to deposit money in a bank on a regular basis. They also need to develop the habit of saving money for larger purchases. (Chapter 8 deals with investments and long-term savings.) These lessons will help your children develop a much more comprehensive understanding of money and how to manage it.

Seven Key Banking Guidelines

The following guidelines may seem basic, but you would be surprised how many adults do not follow them. By introducing them when your children are young, you will start them on the path to achieving financial literacy and independence.

1. Make regular savings a lifelong habit

In chapter 1, "The Allowance Contract," you set up a weekly allowance routine with your children. If you have been following the system, your children have been saving a set portion of their allowance in their piggy banks. This money should be put in a child's savings account.

Set up an account in your child's name where they can make regular deposits of these savings, about once a month. Whatever age you start this with your children, it is good for them to become comfortable going to the bank and to understand that this is an institution that, when used properly, can help them.

2. Let the child do it

Let your child make withdrawals from and deposits to his bank account. Let him fill out the deposit/withdrawal slips, stand in line, and count the money (with your help). Older children will be able to use the bank machine later, but it is important that your young child first learns to deal directly with the bank teller or customer service representative.

Your child needs to develop skills to negotiate money matters directly with people, not machines. Later in life he will also need to negotiate car loans, mortgages, and business financing with people. This step is fundamental to building your child's confidence.

3. Don't pass on the passbook

When you go to the bank to set up an account with your child, get a passbook or "bank book." (Some banks give you the option of a passbook or a monthly statement.) A passbook allows your child to see every deposit and withdrawal as they happen and to hold something that feels real. This experience will heighten her awareness of the banking process.

4. Just say no to bank cards

When you set up your child's bank account, the bank will give you the option of having a bank card. I advise you not to accept it when your children are little. Young children are not ready to use a bank card. They need to understand and be able to handle money in a practical way before advancing to the electronic system.

Bank cards allow children to make transactions without knowing where the money is coming from. For example, when Jeremy was six years old, I told him I did not have any money in my wallet for McDonald's. He told me to get the "free money" from the bank machine!

Bank cards make children's savings too readily available, and they will nickel and dime their savings to nothing. A bank card will also undermine the good savings habits you are trying to foster. Note: bank cards should be introduced to your children when they are in their early teens (see chapter 7).

. . . .

"If you can get kids on the right track at an early age, they're more likely going to be financially successful adults."

Carrie Schwab-Pomerantz, president, Charles Schwab Foundation, quoted in USA Today

. . . .

5. Set a maximum limit on spending money

Even though your child deposits savings in the bank, she may accumulate additional money by saving her spending money as well as gift money. If the amount of money in her wallet gets too large, she should put the excess into the bank as well.

I recommend you set an upper limit in her wallet of about $20 or two weeks' allowance. This amount will be enough money so your child can buy a book, small toy, or movie ticket without needing to make a withdrawal from the bank.

Even when my boys were 15, 13, and 11, they had an upper limit of $20 on money in their wallet. This was set for several reasons. Wallets can get lost, and money can disappear at school or when friends have been over. Also when teens go shopping, there is always the potential for being mugged, or as teens call it, "jumped."

6. Flee from dreaded bank fees

Most banks have special savings accounts for children. These accounts usually have no bank fees. So make sure you open a child's account. If you use a regular adult account, the bank fees could quickly erode the small amount saved by your children. (Learning about bank fees is an important lesson, but not one your child needs to learn at this point.)

7. Put little interest in interest

When I was a child, interest rates on savings accounts were much higher than today. If I received 50 cents in interest, I could spend that money on something substantial. Today, however, interest rates are much lower, and you can't buy much with 50 cents anymore. So do not make a big deal about the interest earned on your children's accounts. At this point, what matters is helping them to make regular savings and build good habits.

The Kid's Bank Money Tracker

Although your child will receive a passbook when you open up the account, it may benefit her to keep her own separate record of the deposits and withdrawals, just as you may do with your

Kid's Bank Money Tracker

Name:			
Date	Deposit	Withdrawal	Balance

Worksheet 3.1

own computer spreadsheet or accounting program. Making a record like this allows your child to get an even better understanding of banking—and provides good math practice as well.

To help your child keep track of their account, use the Kid's Bank Money Tracker (Worksheet 3.1). The form is a simple ledger to keep track of deposits and withdrawals and, of course, the balance in the account.

Banking Tips & Traps

1. **Making the bank appointment:** Before going to the bank to set up your kids' accounts, call the branch and make an appointment. Tell them you are bringing your children and would like to meet with a representative who is good with kids.

2. **Keeping the passbook safe:** As I suggest for your child's wallet, establish a regular, safe place to keep the passbook to avoid losing it. I suggest you keep the passbook yourself, and give it to your kids when they make deposits or withdrawals.

Step-by-Step Summary

1. *Discuss with your child the reasons to open a bank account.*

   These reasons include the following:
   * *to save money for large purchases in the future*
   * *to keep money safe from loss or theft*
   * *to give your child access to their money when and where they need it*

- *to earn money on their savings through interest*
- *to save money for holidays*

2. Set up a bank account.

Go with your child to your local bank branch to open up a bank account. Take the piggy bank, or if the child has a large number of coins, help her count and roll the coins at home. When you open the account, make sure it is a no-fee child's account. Have the bank representative explain the whole process to your child, and have her sign the forms. This is a great learning experience for your child.

3. Make the first deposit.

When you open up the account, deposit the money from the piggy bank. Help your child fill out the deposit slips. When you get the passbook back, look it over with your child. Make deposits on a regular basis, such as monthly. When your child is older (say, 12 or 13), they will be ready to do their banking online—maybe even on their phone. That's also when they can be entrusted with a bank (debit) card (see chapter 7).

4. Have your child keep his own records.

Use the Kid's Bank Money Tracker worksheet on page 60, download it from www.paullermitte.com, or create your own simple spreadsheet. This way, in addition to having a pass-book, your child can record deposits and withdrawals and watch his savings grow.

4

Spending the Bigger Bucks

Teaching your children

- how to be good consumers

- how to make wise buying decisions

- about the relationship between price and quality

IN OUR CONSUMPTION-CRAZED SOCIETY, it is vital to teach our children how to be good consumers. By "good" I mean consumers who make wise, thoughtful buying decisions. Good consumers understand the relationship between quality and price. They research before making major purchases, and they have learned to overcome the urge to spend wildly and impulsively.

Like all life skills, savvy consumerism is a skill best acquired at an early age. That is why I urge parents to let their children spend the bigger bucks on more items, such as expensive toys, clothes, electronics, and sports equipment. Children need to learn from their mistakes. If they buy something on a whim and figure out later they wasted their money, they may be more thoughtful next time. If they buy something of low quality and it breaks down after a few weeks, they may learn to look for better quality. But if you always make the major buying decisions, they will not learn anything, and they will carry this lack of financial expertise into their adult years. So your first step is to let go a little. Let your children spend and learn. Make allowances for them!

A major purchase would be anything priced more than one month's total allowance. For example, if your child is getting $5 per week, a major purchase would be $20 or more. Any purchases below $20 can be made from the money in your child's wallet, while larger purchases should be made from your child's savings in the bank.

REALITY CHECK

During the month, perhaps you can keep part of the allowance money in a safe place at home in case the child's wallet is lost or stolen. Our son Patrick once lost his wallet while we were bowling. He would have lost $35 if his mother had not taken $20 to be put in his bank account. Lucky young man!

Six Key Spending Guidelines

Major purchases need to be made thoughtfully if they are to represent "money well spent." That's a lesson many of us have learned the hard way. However, we can prevent our children from repeating our mistakes if we teach them at a young age the following basic spending guidelines.

1. Plan ahead for major purchases

Spending the bigger bucks on major purchases requires planning and forethought. If your child is interested in buying an expensive toy, for example, encourage her to take some time to think about it. Does she really want the toy? Is there something else she would like to buy instead? If she still wants the toy, perhaps there is a more appropriate model or brand available.

Ideally, every major purchase should be planned over a period of weeks or even months. To help you teach this concept to your children, I created the Wise Purchase Plotter (see worksheet on page 70). This form may help you and your children build a wish list of the things they want to buy, and to track what happens to the item after they purchase it. More on the Wise Purchase Plotter later in the chapter.

2. Do your homework

Before your children make larger purchases, they should do some homework. For example, if they want to buy in-line skates, they should do the following:

- Visit a few different stores to find out the different makes and models.

- Check consumer reports regarding brand quality and safety ratings.

- If possible, research online to compare models and features. (The old-fashioned way, which might still interest young children, is to go through consumer magazines and newspapers and clip out the relevant ads.)

- Talk to friends about what they have. Did their skates last long? Wear well?

- Surf the Web looking for different manufacturers and retailers. Also check prices online for different brands of skates, both new and used (Craigslist, and so on).

- Compare prices. Find out how much each model or brand costs. Determine whether there is a difference in prices from store to store. Find out why some types of skates cost a lot more than others.

- Find out if there are any sales on right now. When is the best time to buy in-line skates? In the spring, or in the fall?

Help your children with this research, but let them do most of the legwork. (This is great bonding time!) Even if they spend half an hour online, it can be very productive. In stores, encourage your children to speak directly to clerks and to ask questions. This process gives them confidence and helps develop their consumer skills as they get older.

REALITY CHECK

Older children can be taught to do the math to figure out and understand the cost of buying items priced in foreign currency. Buying at home can be smarter than buying in another country, because of additional costs such as shipping, customs duty, or taxes.

3. Consider price and quality

While your child is doing the research, explain the relationship between price and quality. In most cases, it is not wise to buy either the cheapest brand or the most expensive. The cheapest is probably of poor quality, and the most expensive brand is likely overpriced, even extravagant. Teach your children the importance of looking at both price and quality.

Teach them to decide what level of quality they want and how much they are willing to pay for it. They also have to understand, paradoxically, that the most costly is not always the best, and the cheapest is not always the worst.

Another buying decision consumers face relates to size or quantity. Talk to your children about reasons to buy the large box of cereal versus the smaller, more expensive one. You could also talk about "buying local" and "buying green."

4. Give your child a month's leeway

As a parent, you should help your child make major purchases and go through the decision-making process with him. However, for smaller purchases, you have to give your child some leeway. I recommend you let your child spend up to a month's allowance without interference. For instance, if your child gets $5 per week in allowance, allow him to accumulate up to $20 in his wallet and to spend it as he chooses. If he has more than $20 in his wallet, the excess funds should be deposited in the bank. This one-month buffer will give your child the opportunity to learn from his experience, either good or bad.

5. Plan ahead for vacations

Trips and vacations can sometimes seriously undermine your allowance system. When you are on a one- or two-week vacation, your children can be constantly asking you to give them money, and the constant pestering can ruin your vacation. You will find yourself saying "No, no, no."

To avoid this scenario, help your children create a spending budget for the vacation. Have them save a specific amount of money (and you can perhaps promise to match this amount). Your children will have this money to buy things on their vacation. You will want to keep some of the money safe for them during the trip, but when your children have their own cash to spend, you do not have to decide what they buy and play the heavy every time you have to say no. Let them make the decisions. And do not stand over them the whole vacation saying, "Don't waste your money on that!"

REALITY CHECK ⤶

On a family vacation, each child saved $100 to bring as spending money. The 13-year-old spent three-quarters of the money; the 11-year-old spent all the money plus more; and the 9-year-old came home with half his money. Each child had a different way of managing money, but they all made their own choices.

However, your children need to understand that you will not be giving them any more money when theirs is spent. To help you with this process, I created the Kid's Vacation Planner worksheet, explained in further detail later in this chapter. Note: by matching their vacation savings, you create a powerful incentive for your children. They may save money by forgoing smaller purchases or by earning more money around the house or neighborhood. In addition, trips abroad are great opportunities to teach your kids about different currencies. If you are planning to visit another country, discuss the difference between the two currencies and how that will affect the amount of money they will have to spend.

6. Teach tipping to reward good service

Your children as consumers need to understand the concept of tipping for good service. If they grasp the concept at an early age, they will learn to make a connection between value and financial reward. This will help them appreciate the hard work of others, and perhaps impress upon them the importance of providing value and service.

When my wife and I went to a restaurant with our young children, we discussed how tipping works and decided together how much we should tip the server. If the service was good, we would leave a tip of about 15 percent, and if the service was poor, we would leave a smaller tip. Most importantly, we discussed the tip together. In this way, our children learned how to show their appreciation for good service and how to judge when the service was inferior. Next time you and your family are out for dinner, have your consumer-smart kids decide on the amount of the tip. (And let them figure out the math!)

The Wise Purchase Plotter

The best way to teach your children to be good consumers is to help them learn from their experience. Think about your own consumer choices. When looking back on purchases you made in the past, you may discover you bought the wrong brand, spent too much money, or purchased something you never use. This experience helps you to be more thoughtful about future purchases.

To help your kids learn from their consumer choices, I've created the Wise Purchase Plotter (Worksheet 4.1). This form helps you and your children track a purchase from beginning to end. It is a helpful tool for teaching children to evaluate their need to purchase, the cost of the item, the differences in quality, and the reason one item may be better than another.

Wise Purchase Plotter

Item	Choices		Cost	Pros	Cons
	1				
	2				
	3				
	1				
	2				
	3				
	1				
	2				
	3				

Worksheet 4.1

You might want to begin using the plotter when your child says she wants to buy something. Have her fill out the worksheet while researching the item and review it one month later. Was she happy with her decision and her purchase? Why or why not? After using the form a few times, your children will acquire a much better sense of what it means to be a good consumer.

The Kid's Vacation Planner

The Kid's Vacation Planner is designed to help your kids save and/or earn enough spending money for a vacation. As explained earlier, it is better for your kids to have their own spending money on a vacation. Starting to save when you begin planning the vacation, months in advance, will give your children plenty of time to get together enough money for the trip.

Spending Tips & Traps

1. **Allow your child to make mistakes:** Try not to control the whole process or make all of the buying decisions for your children.

2. **Model good consumer behavior:** If you make spontaneous buying decisions, your kids will learn to do the same. If you want your kids to be good consumers, you will have to be one yourself.

3. **Go out for dinner and teach your children about tipping:** Let your children assess the service and decide on the tip. Remember to let them know that when they are older, they might have a job waiting on tables. So they need to be good consumers and reward the server for a job well done.

Kid's Vacation Planner

Destination	
Departure Date	
Dollar Goal	
Weekly Contribution	

Date	Deposit	Total

Worksheet 4.2

Step-by-Step Summary

1. **Review the Allowance Contract you signed with your children.**

   In the contract they listed what they would use their savings for. Review the list together. Is it relevant? Add new items for consideration.

2. **When planning for family vacations, discuss the vacation spending plan with your children.**

   Offer to match their savings. Use the Kid's Vacation Planner to help your children save for the trip.

3. **Talk about consumer concepts, such as brands, features, buying local, and buying green.**

   Help your child plan ahead for major purchases and do consumer research. Discuss the relationship between price and quality, giving specific examples your children can relate to. Set a one-month spending limit for bigger items (equal to one month's allowance).

4. **Identify a potential purchase.**

   When your child chooses a bigger-ticket item to buy, explain how it will be paid for. Use the Wise Purchase Plotter to record three spending options, with their pros and cons.

5. **Research a potential purchase.**

   Help your children gather information about the item they wish to buy. This might include visiting stores to compare prices and quality, and reading consumer reports. Such steps will help your child make the "best buy" and also feel confident about their purchase.

6. **Make the decision to buy or not to buy.**

   After researching options, decide with your child whether or not to buy the item at all and, secondly, which brand to purchase. Use the Wise Purchase Plotter to compare choices, and make the purchase with your child.

7. **Assess the wisdom of the purchase.**

   After three months, review the Wise Purchase Plotter worksheet again. Discuss the purchase with your child. Was it a good purchase? Why or why not?

5

The Case of the Broken Window

Teaching your children

- respect for their own property and the property of other people

- appropriate behavior in other people's homes and in restaurants, hotels, and other environments

Strategies for parents

- establish a consistent policy of consequences should your children violate a property rule

IT WAS BOUND to happen. Your child just smashed the neighbor's front window while playing ball. Your neighbor is really upset, your kid is upset, and now you are upset. In this situation, what do you do? Pay to have the window replaced out of your own funds, or have your child pay for it with his allowance? Was it an accident, or should you discipline your child for being careless or deliberately destructive?

There are no easy answers to these questions, which makes it even more important to establish rules with your children about property rights. That way, when your child breaks a window or shatters Aunt Nellie's china teapot, you'll know what to do, and your child will know what to expect. And hopefully, when your child reaches adulthood, he will have a healthy respect for his own property and the property of others.

Now Is the Time to Start

When your children reach five or six years of age, they start spreading their wings. They become more physically active, more curious, and more experimental. They also become susceptible to the early stages of peer pressure. Under these circumstances, even the most angelic child will probably break something valuable. She will also lose things, find things, or even try her hand at stealing or vandalism.

At this stage, you have a choice. You can discipline your child for every infraction or develop a more subtle, graduated method of dealing with your child's early forays into the world of property rights. I suggest the second method, because I do not believe children should be disciplined simply for being children.

Your children should be allowed to make mistakes and learn from them. If they take responsibility for their actions, in some cases kids should be rewarded, not disciplined. In fact, I think children should be disciplined only if they persist in their disregard for property rights. The key, of course, is to set the rules and teach them to your children.

The Rules of Property Rights

In our family, we established guidelines regarding property rights early on. Over the years, we used these rules to sort out all kinds of situations. For example, jumping or walking on the sofa means you sit on the floor. Stealing from a store means the child returns the item to the store owner. Breaking your brother's possession means you must help to pay to replace it.

Here is a summary of my suggested family policy with respect to property rights:

1. Everyone can make mistakes—even parents.

2. It is not a crime to make mistakes; it is only a crime not to learn from them.

3. Look after your property. Do not break it, bash it, trash it, or forget it.

4. Look after other people's property as if it were your own.

5. If you break it, fix it. If you lose it, replace it.

6. Take responsibility for your mistakes. If you did it, admit it.

7. If you make the same mistake twice, you are going to help pay for it.

8. If you find something, turn it in.

9. Keep your bedroom neat and tidy. It need not be a jungle.

Nine Key Property Rights Guidelines

The rules outlined above will help your children through many difficult situations—and possibly keep them out of trouble, too. Internalizing and adhering to these simple virtues will help them throughout their lives. When you as a parent are enforcing these rules, keep the following guidelines in mind.

1. Make allowances for your kids

Do not discipline your children just because they are children. Remember, everyone makes mistakes. Allow your children some grace. Only discipline them if they continue to exhibit the same negative behavior. For example, when one of our sons was six years old, he took a comic book from a store without paying for it. He did a bad thing, but he did not realize he had done anything wrong.

Instead of punishing or berating him, I took him back to the store, had him apologize to the owner, and then I paid for the comic book. I also made my son understand the possibly grave consequences of stealing, and he got the message. He has never stolen anything again.

If he had continued to steal, of course, I would have disciplined him. I would also have looked for contributing factors—had he been seeking attention more than usual or comparing himself to a new set of friends? This story illustrates the most important concept about kids and property: You have to "make allowances" for your children. Let them make mistakes—once or twice—without severe consequences, and only clamp down if they fail to learn from the lesson. Show acceptance and love, and help them understand what the correct behavior is.

2. Use discretion and subtlety

When children break property rules, which can certainly happen with friends, at school, or in families, base your response on the specific context of the situation. If your child accidentally breaks something, you probably should not discipline him. For example, if your child is telling an exciting story at the dinner table and knocks his glass over onto the floor, and it breaks, this is obviously an accident. However, if he is throwing a football in the house and breaks a lamp, knowing that one of the house rules is "No throwing balls in the house," the child should be disciplined to some degree.

A child can help repair or replace broken items. If they have broken something for a second time (through mischief or carelessness) or broken a household rule, the child can pay for the cost of replacement. As I have said, if the behavior persists, the form of discipline should be increased for each infraction. Use your discretion to decide what is appropriate in each circumstance.

When your children break a property rule, ask them to decide what would be an appropriate form of discipline.

3. Teach accountability and responsibility

Get your kids involved in caring for things they use regularly. Show them how to do basic activities such as the following:

- maintain their bikes

- wash the car

- paint the fence

- polish their dress shoes

- sew a button on a shirt or blouse

These are life skills that translate into care of property. And they teach a valuable life lesson: The cost of maintenance is lower than the cost of replacement.

REALITY CHECK

There are many ways children can get involved in caring for their property. Our kids painted their playhouse when they were three and five years old! They cleaned their soccer boots after each game. And once a week they gave their bedrooms a thorough tidy-up.

4. Make your kids pay the second time around

In most cases, your child should only pay for something broken or lost the second or third time they have made the same mistake. The first time, the parent should pay for it. The second time, you can decide how much your child should contribute to the cost of replacing or fixing the property—based on age, the rules ignored, and the circumstances. The amount will be based on your levels of discipline and on the ability of your child to pay, as well as the replacement or repair cost of the particular item.

REALITY CHECK ⮐

During a period of five years, each of our children broke one of the glass panes on our front door. We paid the repair bill, but they knew that the next time a pane was broken, the bill would be paid by the one who broke it.

5. Do not withhold allowance as a disciplinary measure

If you decide your child should pay for a damaged or lost item, do not take it out of her allowance. Require your child to earn the money by working around the house or neighborhood. The experience of working off the debt will reinforce the lesson she learned from the experience. And it will help to keep nagging down and savings up.

6. Discuss the consequences with your child

When your children break a property rule, ask them to decide what would be an appropriate form of discipline. If they come up with the consequence themselves, they will be more likely to learn from the experience as well. Of course, the disciplinary measure will have to be close to what you would have decided. If your child comes up with too lax a consequence, you can tell him what the "real" consequence will be.

7. Start with the child's bedroom

Respect for property begins at home. If your children can develop respect for their own property, they will more likely show the same respect for others' property. So start by helping your children keep their rooms tidy. Kids or teenagers—they all need a little help! Do not let them leave their clothes and toys lying all over the place. Have them make their beds and do some

Kid's Inventory

Name:					
√	I Have	√	I Need	√	I Want

Worksheet 5.1

basic cleaning. Provide them with shelves and drawers for their belongings.

If your kids develop good habits in their own domains, these will translate into greater respect for property in all aspects of their lives. And the cost of items for your home and your children should be reduced because these items are being better cared for.

* * *

"Young children are rarely self-disciplined enough to work alone. They love to work with us. So make toy pickup a joint task...."

Kathy Lynn, parenting expert,
www.parentingtoday.ca

* * *

8. Teach the Golden Rule

When your child shows disregard for someone else's personal property, teach him the Golden Rule—that he should always treat others as he would like others to treat him. Ask him if he would like it if someone broke *his* toy or stole *his* baseball cards. Help your children to see the relationship between the feelings they have for their stuff and how other people feel about their own things. This is especially useful when your child finds some-thing and wants to keep it. Ask her: "If you lost something, would you want the finder to keep it or return it to you?" If you ask her this question, she will probably realize quickly that she should try to find the rightful owner.

9. Have your kids take a personal inventory

Your kids may have a lot of stuff stashed all over the house. They probably own things they have forgotten about or tend to neglect their property because they have so much. To instill in your children a sense of ownership and pride in their possessions, help them take a personal inventory. Have each child make a list of all of their major possessions.

This exercise helps kids take greater pride in their possessions and also helps them appreciate how fortunate they are. You can use the Kid's Inventory (Worksheet 5.1) or create a simple chart to complete this task. Similar to your own insurance inventory, kids might want to include key information, such as colour, brand, and serial number, of major items such as bicycles—or even take a photo inventory. They could also make a list of "needs" and "wants."

REALITY CHECK ⇤

A good time for your children to take an inventory of their possessions is after Christmas, after a birthday, or during summer holidays, when many new things are in their rooms. Any of these times is a good time to think about giving things away or holding a garage sale. Our family held a garage sale once, and the kids all helped. We raised enough money to buy something we all wanted.

Reinforce Property Rights Before Special Events

Before going with your children to a restaurant, a hotel, or a friend's house, have a short conversation just before entering the new place. Ask your kids, "What is considered good behavior when we are in a [fill in the blank]?" In my experience this short discussion "in the moment" translates into much better respect for property and results in a much more enjoyable visit for everyone. This is especially appropriate for children ages four to nine; after that, they probably know how to behave and do not need a reminder.

Teaching your kids about property rights will take months, perhaps years. However, if you consistently reinforce a specific policy in your family, your children will grow up with a well-developed respect for other people and their property.

Step-by-Step Summary

1. **Discuss the concept of property rights with your children.**

   Spend some time with your kids talking about
   * *respect for their own property*
   * *respect for the property of other people*
   * *what will happen if they make a mistake and break or lose something*
   * *what will happen if they do not learn from their mistake and instead continue to break the rules*
   * *how and when they will help pay to replace or fix property*
   * *what they should do if they find something that does not belong to them*
   * *other rules relating to property, including no-no's such as stealing and vandalism*

2. **Set rules for your kids' bedrooms.**

   Provide guidelines for a tidy room, and decide on the consequences of a messy room. Setting a regular day and time for a weekly cleanup can be very helpful to keep bedrooms from "going wild."

3. **Have your children complete the Kid's Inventory worksheet.**

   Go through your children's belongings with them (don't forget the storage locker or garage!). Have them list their major possessions, and teach them to care for these possessions. Help them set aside unused and unwanted items to give to charity or sell in a garage sale.

4. **Before a special event, talk to your children about appropriate behavior.**

   Ask them to describe the proper way to behave at a [fill in the blank]. For younger kids especially, remind them of your expectations and the consequences for inappropriate behavior.

- -

**Children often have a treasure
trove of clothes and toys that
they have outgrown or abandoned.**

- -

6

The Gift of Giving

Teaching your children

- how to give from their hearts

- how to contribute to their community

Strategies for parents

- create a family system for regular
  charitable giving

LIKE ALL THE GOOD HABITS discussed in this book, the art of giving is a skill that is best learned at a tender age. To lead a meaningful life, all of us need to learn to give back something of ourselves to the world.

In my family, I have tried to teach my children the joy of contributing to their community, through both time and money. Each month, my boys gave a portion of their allowance to the church. They were involved in helping with community organizations. They also gave away their unwanted clothes and toys. These experiences taught them how satisfying it is to do something worthwhile for others. They learned how to give from their hearts, not just out of a sense of duty or obligation.

They also learned to look outward to the world, not just inward to their own needs. Building relationships with people beyond their own circle helps children to see the bigger picture, and as adults they will be more empathetic. Teaching the gift of giving is an important way to instill a sense of balance in our children about money, material possessions, and the greater experience of life and relationships.

REALITY CHECK ⏎

The grandma in one family I know sends a package of baking to her great-grandchildren every Christmas. When it arrives, it is always joyfully received. One year, the children sent their usual letter of thanks, but this time they went into their piggy banks and added some of their own money to the letter as a special gift to Great-grandma. They were so excited to send this special thank-you. Her reply came in the mail: "Thank you so much for thinking of me. May God bless you for your generosity. Remember, it is better to give than to receive. Love, Great-grandma." With the letter was a big, beautiful box of chocolates. (This woman knows the language of children!)

Seven Key Giving Guidelines

To teach your kids the gift of giving, I recommend you start a system for regular donations, of both time and money. While the particulars will be unique to you and your family (such as what charities and community groups you choose), the system should follow these general guidelines.

1. Give a set percentage of your income to charity

When your children have learned to handle their allowance, by putting regular savings in the bank, they are ready to put aside a specific amount for charities. As a starting point, they could contribute 5 to 10 percent of their allowance to a charity every month. The actual amount could be higher or lower, as long as the percentage is consistent.

2. Give to charity on a regular basis

Your children will learn the gift of giving more effectively if they make their contributions on a regular basis, perhaps once a month. I recommend the contribution be made to the same charity at least for the first year or two. Examples include children's charities, environmental groups, children's hospitals, animal shelters, and food banks.

3. Give to a local charity

For your children to learn the gift of giving, they need to see firsthand the positive results of their generosity. That is why I recommend they give to a charity in your community. If they can actually see the people they are helping and the positive results, they will experience more profoundly the joy of giving. Giving a gift of time or money in person beats making a quick, anonymous donation online. Local charitable giving can also open up important discussions and lead to understanding (or education) that is more global in nature.

4. Get your kids involved physically

While it is important for them to give financially, it is also meaningful for your children to give of their time. Find a community project or organization that needs volunteers—for starters, your local food bank, thrift store, or animal shelter—and get your kids to sign up. If you want, you can participate as well. (Your assistance may be mandatory if your children are younger.) Talk about volunteers and what they do in your community and around the world. This is also a great opportunity for your kids to experience giving as an independent activity.

5. Help your kids choose an organization they can relate to

If your kids love dogs and cats, get them involved with the local animal shelter. If they love the outdoors, get them to join a local natural history group, streamkeepers, or "friends of a park." If they like learning, perhaps they can volunteer to teach other kids. The more interested they are in a particular area, the more likely they will be to enjoy giving their time.

6. Help your children to give their gifts

When it comes time to buy gifts for birthdays and special occasions, help your children buy their own. Do not do it for them. You can give them the money for the present, but they should buy it themselves. Let's say your son needs to buy a birthday present for a friend. You can take him to the store and help him find something, or you can give him $10, $15, or $20 and tell him to find something on his own.

Either way, your child will learn how to select gifts and how it feels to give a present that took some time to find. In each case, you will provide the money, but your child will do the legwork.

Giving a gift of time or money in person beats making a quick, anonymous donation online.

Note: I don't think children should have to pay for gifts until they are about 12 years old. At 12 years of age, children are more able to earn extra money through babysitting, refereeing, doing yard work, and delivering papers. With this new source of cash, the child may want to buy presents independently. Older children may decide they want to give on their own.

REALITY CHECK

One family I know has a $10 limit for gifts for siblings at Christmastime. Hints are dropped, and snooping is done to find something meaningful for the other person. Parents give suggestions and help the younger ones make purchases. Such a system helps to keep budgets in check at Christmas.

7. Give away unused clothes and toys

Children often have a treasure trove of clothes and toys that they have outgrown or abandoned. It is a great exercise to have them sort through their stuff and pick out the things they do not need anymore. Take your kids to a local agency such as a women's shelter, children's hospital, or parent resource center and have them personally hand over the articles. (You might want to phone first to determine what items are needed.) Your kids will discover how satisfying it is to help other people in this way, and they will be keeping their rooms cleaner at the same time. It may also help them realize that there really *is* such a thing as "too much," and that more stuff does not necessarily make you happier.

Positive Blessings Worksheet

Name:	
Things I Am Grateful For	Things I Can Give to Others

Worksheet 6.1

Worksheets and Exercises

Positive Blessings Worksheet

The first step in learning the gift of giving is to appreciate how lucky you are. The more your children count their blessings, the more they will be inclined to give to the outside world. To help your kids take stock of their good fortune, help them complete a Positive Blessings Worksheet opposite. Here they can list the things for which they are grateful and then list the things that they will give. This exercise helps your kids literally count their blessings.

Gift of Giving Contract

If you want your kids to give on a regular, consistent basis, they need to plan ahead. Help your children fill out the Gift of Giving Contract (Worksheet 6.2). Have them each decide on three ways they can help other people. For example, they can choose:

- a local organization to give money to (and how much money to give)

- a community group, to support as a volunteer

- a charity to which they will donate unused clothes and toys

REALITY CHECK

One way to give is to plan a trip to the grocery store once a month. After your child pays for her treats, she can drop a coin (or coins) in the box or tin by the checkout; many charities have donation boxes there. You could also purchase non-perishables to give to the food bank.

Gift of Giving Contract

Three Ways I Can Help Others

Money

I will donate $_____ per week to the following local charity or organization:

_____

Time

I will donate my time to the following community group or organization:

_____

Time per week/month/year: _____

Clothes and Toys

I will donate unused clothes and toys to the following local charity
or organization:

_____

_____

Child

_____

Date

Worksheet 6.2

Giving Tips & Traps

1. **Let your kids do it themselves:** With your help, let your children choose their charity and community projects. Let them do much of the work themselves.

2. **Keep it in your community:** Keep all of your charity or volunteer projects as local as possible. The interaction with their local community will give your children the best experience possible.

3. **Help your children to be consistent:** Use the Gift of Giving Contract provided in this chapter to keep your kids on track with their giving. Regular giving is as important as regular saving.

4. **Get the kids involved in something they like:** You want them to enjoy the project for which they are volunteering and have a positive first experience as volunteers. This will give them the idea that giving can be fun and also helpful.

5. **Plan ahead for emergency giving:** Disasters such as floods, earthquakes, and famines can make children and families want to help. Your children may wish to set aside some of their charitable money for this purpose. Especially when donating money to overseas aid, assist reputable organizations with a strong track record. See the Resources section for a list of such groups.

Step-by-Step Summary

1. Decide on the charity.

Help your child choose a charity. Make it local, if possible, and make it relate to a personal interest.

2. **Determine the amount of giving.**

   Help your children decide how much to donate each month. I suggest 5 to 10 percent of their allowance each month. It's important to be consistent. For older children, the Internet has made charitable giving very easy to research and accomplish.

3. **Have your child choose and volunteer for a project.**

   Help your child volunteer for a local community project or organization. They could volunteer for a short- or long-term project.

4. **Give unwanted clothes and toys to charity.**

   Help your kids sort through their belongings on a regular basis. Go with them to take unwanted items to a local charity. Have them give their boxes of stuff to volunteers.

5. **Complete a Positive Blessings Worksheet.**

   Have your kids write down things they are thankful for. Discuss how and why others are unfortunate. Discuss ways your family can help.

6. **Complete the Gift of Giving Contract.**

   List the three ways your kids plan to help in the community. Use the worksheet to identify regular donations and volunteering.

The Debit Side
of the Coin

. . . .

Teaching your children

- how to use a debit card properly

- to maintain good savings habits even while using a debit card

- to make well-considered consumer choices even when money is readily accessible

. . . .

ALTHOUGH DEBIT CARDS have become extremely common in Western economies, real dollars and cents are still the best tools for teaching your kids about money. By handling dimes, quarters, and paper bills, your children learn about money in a tangible and much more comprehensive way.

If your children use a debit card for most transactions and rarely handle cash, there is a danger that they will not learn important lessons about handling money. They could start using the bank machine like they use the refrigerator. When they are hungry to buy something, they will simply dip into the bank machine. They might eat up their savings by buying whatever strikes their fancy in the moment. All of the good habits you have been trying to teach them might get tossed aside once they get their hands on that little piece of plastic.

And there is one more potential danger. If your child gets hooked on a debit card, it could lead to "harder stuff": credit cards, store cards, frivolous consumer loans, and other forms of floating credit. In other words, the debit card could set your child off in the wrong direction.

In spite of these debit card pitfalls, we as parents have to be realistic. We are moving toward a cashless future when most transactions will involve the transfer of electronic funds over the Web. Almost every purchase—including houses, haircuts, and hamburgers—will be made electronically. Instead of fleeing from these technological changes, we need to figure out how we can help our children grow up to be financially responsible adults in a cashless society.

That is the great opportunity facing you as a parent. You can teach your children how to set their own limits on spending even if the funds are readily available with a simple swipe of a card. You can also teach them how to become comfortable with money as a virtual symbol rather than as a tangible commodity.

Experts tell us that children begin to think more abstractly as they reach ten years of age. Therefore, I encourage you to wait until your child reaches at least ten (and some kids may need to wait longer) before providing them with a debit card. This will emphasize to them the responsibility and privilege that comes with this technology. Using the principles and approach in this chapter, you can teach your children how to use debit cards responsibly, a skill that will be extremely useful in their adult years.

This chapter sets out eight key debit guidelines you can follow as you teach your children about responsible debit card use.

Your children must show they understand how to use a debit card properly before they get to use one independently.

Eight Key Debit Guidelines

Teaching your kids good money habits using debit cards instead of cash is a tricky business. As I've said, all of the good money-management habits they have acquired so far could be jeopardized by that little card. So you have to proceed carefully. Here are some guidelines for the use of debit cards.

1. Encourage responsible use of the debit card

As mentioned, try not to introduce the debit card to your children until age ten, even if their friends have one (and your kids will want them!). You have to make sure they understand the rules of the road. Treat a debit card like a driver's license. Your children must show they understand how to use a debit card properly before they get to use one independently.

To start the process, begin by keeping the card for your child. Only let him use the card in your presence. That will give you the chance to discuss the dangers and opportunities presented by the card when he is using it. The most important concepts to teach your children are as follows:

- They should stick to their good money habits even if they have the card.

- They should still plan their purchases ahead of time. If they have not set a goal for a major purchase, they should not use the debit card to buy something on the spur of the moment.

- If they are not careful, the card might tempt them to buy a lot more than they can afford, which will eat up their savings.

- Bank machines are not refrigerators. They should not go to the bank machine every time they want something.

- They should use the card to make deposits and withdrawals on a regular basis—an average of once a week, or even once a month.

- To keep track of deposits and withdrawals, they could start an accounts book, use a checkbook balance system, or perhaps check the account online (with appropriate supervision).

2. Set limits on use of the card

Teach your children to set limits on how often they use the card and how much they can withdraw at a time. I suggest you limit each of your children to one purchase or withdrawal per week, especially at the start. Make it clear: they should not be running off to the bank machine every time they are out of cash.

3. Use control mechanisms

Fortunately, it's possible to set limits on the debit card when you get it from the bank. You can set the card to:

• accept only deposits, not withdrawals or purchases

• limit the daily amount of withdrawals (to only $20 per day, for example)

• limit the amount of point-of-sale purchases (such as $100 per day)

These limits can be changed as your children begin to demonstrate responsible use of the debit card.

**Using a debit card wisely
is one of the most important skills
your children need to learn
about money in our modern society.**

4. Get the right kind of card

Different financial institutions offer different kinds of debit cards. I suggest you find a debit card that charges no transaction fees. (Some institutions will waive the fees on debit cards and savings accounts for children.)

5. Do not use direct deposit

Although many adults have their salaries deposited directly into their bank account, avoid transferring your children's allowances from your account to their accounts. Keep giving them cash. Have them maintain the same routine you started in chapter 1 with the Allowance Contract. You still want them to make their own deposits so they can learn from this activity.

When your children are in their teens, you can start the process of direct deposit. Good money habits should be in place by then. Younger children need the tangible use of money to comprehend its value. This was the advice I gave to one of our friends who wanted to have the bank automatically deposit money into their children's accounts each month. Even though doing so would save you time and hassle, resist this virtual transaction for your younger children (and some teens). Direct deposit could prevent your children from learning good money habits they will need for the future.

6. Use only short-term savings accounts

It is best to have only one account (the short-term savings account) accessible by the debit card. You do not want your children using the debit card to withdraw money from their medium- or long-term savings. That is a recipe for financial meltdown. Have the bank put medium-term savings into rolling 30-day term deposits to safeguard the money. Have your children put their long-term savings into mutual funds.

7. Keep some cash in their wallets

Even though they have a debit card, your children should still keep some cash in their wallets or purses. I suggest a maximum of $20. This is enough for a week's activities yet not too much to lose. This amount may vary from family to family; what is important is to set a limit on the amount of cash your children carry.

8. Improve security with a debit card

Better safety and security is one major benefit of a debit card over cash. A debit card can protect your children much better than cash against loss and theft. To improve this level of safety, here are a few commonsense suggestions:

- Limit the amount of daily withdrawals and purchases.

- Teach your children to keep the existence of the cards and their personal identification numbers (PINs) to themselves.

- Tell your children to avoid flashing their money in public places.

- Warn your children to be careful at the ATM, screening their PIN and staying aware of their surroundings.

- To avoid extra service charges, they should try to use their own bank's ATMs rather than those located in convenience stores or at restaurants.

- It may also be safer to use only indoor bank machines, rather than those located outside, and to avoid using them after dark.

Keep an Eye on the Future

If there is one thing we have learned about technology, we know it is always changing. Just when we get used to bank machines and debit cards, a new way to spend money electronically comes along. Within a few years, we will see the emergence of smart cards, which store funds in a computer chip on the card. You will be able to use these cards for parking meters, vending machines, and just about anything else you can imagine. You will also be able to download funds onto your smart card from your bank account over the Internet or through a card reader on your telephone. We are getting ever closer to the cashless society. And hopefully, the lessons you teach your children about debit cards will help them to be good money managers even when dollars give way to bits and bytes.

Using a debit card wisely is one of the most important skills your children need to learn about money in our modern society. If you take the time now to teach your children how to use a debit card properly, their know-how will prevent a financial and emotional drain on you today and in the future. In addition, your children will be much better equipped to prosper in the twenty-first century, when dollars and cents may be just the whimsical interest of historians and antique collectors.

Step-by-Step Summary

1. **Discuss the pros and cons of debit cards with your children.**

   Explain how debit cards work and the rules for using them. Begin by allowing your children to use the card only in your presence.

2. **Go to the bank.**

   When your child is ready to sign up for a debit card, accompany them to the bank.

3. **Choose the right debit card.**

   If possible, find a debit card that has no transaction fees.

4. **Choose the limits on the card.**

   Ask the bank to set limits on the amount that can be withdrawn or used for purchases on any given day. Limit access on the card to your child's short-term savings account.

5. **Have your child keep some cash.**

   Encourage your child to keep a maximum amount of cash on hand. I have suggested $20 earlier, but each family will need to decide what is right for them.

6. **Limit card use to once per week.**

   You can give the card to your child once a week and have them return it to you after they have used it. When they are older and also more responsible, you need not hold their card(s) for them.

7. **Review goals and priorities with your child.**

   Reinforce the importance of sticking to the long-term savings plan (see next chapter) even though money is more easily accessible using the debit card.

Decision-making skills are important in all areas of life, but they are especially important in the world of money.

8

Building the
Money Mountain

Teaching your children

- how to make better choices about spending money

- the basics of budgeting

- the importance of long-term savings

MY DEFINITION of financial maturity is simple: it is the ability to give up instant gratification in order to realize long-term dreams and goals. It is the maturity to recognize that big goals do not happen on their own; they require small sacrifices every day. After your children have learned the basics of handling money, they should expand their money-management skills to incorporate long-term savings.

Six Key Savings Guidelines

As a parent, it is vitally important for you to teach your children how to build a "money mountain." They must learn how to create a simple budget and how to divide their money into short-, medium-, and long-term funds. In so doing, they will hone their decision-making skills. They will learn how to decide how much money to spend today, how much to save for a large purchase or a vacation, and how much to invest in long-term savings such as a mutual fund. If your children have absorbed the previous concepts in this book, they will be ready to take this step. Here are my savings guidelines for you and your family.

1. Teach your children budgeting basics

Budgeting and cash flow management are big words, especially when you are 10 or 11 years old. But they are actually very simple concepts. A budget helps you decide how you will spend the money you receive on a regular basis (weekly, monthly, annually). Cash flow management helps you put your money in the right places so you will have enough for everything you want to do.

Both of these concepts are important for your children to learn at an early age—a process aided by use of the Kid's Cash Flow Worksheet. Learning how to budget and manage their cash will take many years, but by starting at a young age, your children

Kid's Cash Flow Worksheet

	Monthly	Annual
Income		
Allowance		
Gift money		
Work money		
Expenses		
Entertainment		
Lunches / Snacks		
Movies		
Video games		
Day spas		
Hobbies / School		
Magazines		
Music		
School activities		
Gifts		
Birthdays		
Special occasions		
Transportation		
Bus fare		
Vacation		
Savings		
Miscellaneous		

Worksheet 8.1

will be well equipped to manage their money properly when they reach their late teens and early twenties.

2. Help your children set financial goals

Having a goal makes all the difference in managing money. If you have a long-term goal in mind, you are more motivated to make day-to-day sacrifices in order to achieve it. Without a goal, you may spend money frivolously and never save anything for a rainy day. So your challenge is to teach your kids how to set goals for their money. The goals themselves are not so important; it is the act of setting goals that is key. (More on goal setting in chapter 9.)

3. Teach your children the fine art of choosing

Because the number of things we want to buy is infinite, and money is usually finite, making choices is the only answer. And how well we make choices can greatly affect our future. Good decision-making skills need to be learned: how to list options, how to compare them, how to make a decision, and how to live with that decision. Of course, decision-making skills are important in all areas of life, but they are especially important in the world of money.

At this stage, your children should learn they have to think about where they want to put their money. Do they want to spend it all today or save it for a new skateboard? Do they want to save it for a vacation next month or put it into a mutual fund? If they can develop their decision-making skills early on, they will make better decisions as adults.

4. Divide money into distinct categories

Teach your kids to divide their money into three areas:

- *Short-term money* for things such as candies, comics, movies, snacks, and other small purchases. Approximately 5 to 10 percent of this category should be allotted to charity.

- *Medium-term money* for larger purchases such as vacations, toys, sports equipment or clothes.

- *Long-term money* to invest in mutual funds or other investments, as well as for larger purchases such as a car, university, or a dream vacation.

Help your kids understand the difference between short- and medium-term money. Short-term money can be held in their wallets, while medium-term money is saved in their bank accounts until they need it. This money is saved from their allowances and from doing odd jobs, as discussed in chapter 1. When creating their budgets, help them decide how much money to put into each category. Use the Kid's Budget Planner (page 113) to get started. For example, you could divide the money as follows:

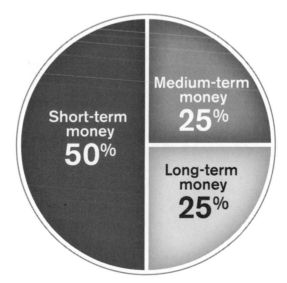

While it is probably quite easy for your kids to save their money in the bank for large expenses like vacations or sports equipment, it is quite another matter for them to save their money for the long term. When a child is ten years old, the idea of saving money just for the sake of it can sound almost ludicrous. "What's the point of putting your money in the bank if you never take it out?" your daughter may ask. At this point, you have to explain the value of building a "money mountain."

When your kids are making decisions about money (what to buy and when), it is important that they view the process as a positive one.

Some children will want to spend 100 percent of their money on short-term gratification. That is why they need to have goals and dreams to save for. Each family and each child may determine different percentages, but the emphasis will remain the same. Also, if your child is saving for a specific item or event, she may put up to 75 percent toward it. Talk with your child so that she can learn from experience.

Kid's Budget Planner

First Month			
Week	Short-Term Amount	Medium-Term Amount	Long-Term Amount
1.			
2.			
3.			
4.			

Second Month			
Week	Short-Term Amount	Medium-Term Amount	Long-Term Amount
1.			
2.			
3.			
4.			

Third Month			
Week	Short-Term Amount	Medium-Term Amount	Long-Term Amount
1.			
2.			
3.			
4.			

Worksheet 8.2

5. Discuss the concept of the "money mountain"

The benefits of long-term savings (from the perspective of a 10-year-old) are as follows:

- You will earn money on your money (interest).

- Your mountain will start getting bigger and bigger, faster and faster (compound interest).

- You will own part of many different companies (mutual fund or share ownership).

- You will be able to use these funds for really important things, like attending college, buying a car, or going on a great trip.

When your kids are making decisions about money (what to buy and when), it is important that they view the process as a positive one. Instead of looking at money as something they just spend as it comes along, budgeting will allow them to look ahead and decide beforehand how they want to divide up the money that will be coming. The habit of looking ahead, instead of from day to day, is an extremely important money-management skill that should be learned early in life.

REALITY CHECK

Early in 1998, we had a family discussion about the Olympics to be held in Australia in 2000. Jan and I had talked about going to Australia since we were first married, and the kids were excited about seeing the Olympics live because they dreamed of one day participating in track and field or soccer at an Olympic level. We agreed that getting to the Olympics was a goal we all wanted to work toward, so we started to put medium- and long-term savings away for that special trek. We saved for two years and got the kids saving too.

---

6. Get professional advice

When your children are ready to begin putting money into long-term investments, I suggest you seek out a professional advisor. If you have your own financial advisor, they will probably be the ideal person to work with. Go with your children to meet with the advisor, and have your advisor explain the basics of investments. This will give your children some experience dealing with professional advisors and will establish in their minds how investments are different from putting money in the bank.

7. Open a mutual fund account in your child's name

Discuss the nature of mutual funds and the reasons for investing in them. Help your child track their investments using a simple spreadsheet or the Kid's Investment Calculator worksheet (next page). By recording information from each statement, she will see the value of the fund go up and down over time, depending on stock market conditions.

Of course, budgets and investments need periodic review. After six months, you should review with your child their earlier budget. Was it realistic? Did your child spend more or less than they expected in each category? This is a great time to consider and evaluate spending choices—and revisit the benefits of long-term saving. You can discuss how the budget might be adjusted and create a new one for the next six or twelve months.

Kid's Investment Calculator

Date	Amount	Source (Allowance, Job, Gift)	Cumulative* Savings Total

*The term cumulative *refers here to total savings accumulated over time.*
To calculate cumulative savings, add any new amount to the previous total.

Worksheet 8.3

Step-by-Step Summary

1. **Explain how a budget works.**

   Talk with your children about why they need to create a budget, using the Kid's Cash Flow Worksheet as a start. Stress that a budget will allow your children to have enough money for the things they want, while saving money for the future.

2. **Establish a goal or goals.**

   Help your child set some financial goals over the medium term and long term. List some things she would like to save for over the next six months to a year (vacation, new bike, sports equipment) and what she would like to save for over a period of years (college, a car, an extended trip).

3. **Explain how to divide money into three categories.**

   Help your child understand the three categories of money (short term, medium term, and long term).

4. **Decide how much to allocate to each category.**

   Help your child to determine the distribution across the categories. I suggest:

   - *50% for short-term needs*
   - *25% for medium-term needs*
   - *25% for long-term savings*

5. **Create a budget.**

   Help your child to create a budget for allocation of funds over the next six months or perhaps the school year. In the Kid's Budget Planner worksheet, enter the amounts that will be allocated each week in the three categories. Add up the planned expenditures in the short term. Indicate the expenditures planned for the medium-term category. Add up the money that will be invested in long-term savings over the six-month period.

6. **Meet with your financial advisor.**

   Go with your child to visit your financial advisor. Have your advisor explain how mutual funds work and how they differ from savings accounts. Open a mutual fund account in your child's name.

7. **Help your child track their investments.**

   Create a spreadsheet or use the Kid's Investment Calculator worksheet to record your child's investment in mutual funds. Each time he receives a statement, he can record the value of the fund. In this way, he can see how the value of his investment goes up and down depending on conditions in the market.

8. **Review the past budget and make a new budget.**

   At the end of six months, sit down with your child and review the success of the previous budget. Discuss how to do the budget differently. Fill out a new budget for the next six or twelve months.

9

The Lifetime Goal Formula

Teaching your children

- to set lifetime goals

- to have the confidence to strive for their goals

- to identify their true instincts, abilities, and passions

IT IS ACCEPTED WISDOM that goal setting is the cornerstone of sound financial planning. When we plan ahead, we will find it easier to forgo immediate gratification and avoid spur-of-the-moment mistakes. If your kids have been diligently working with you on the concepts in this book, they are probably getting good at setting goals for themselves—not just financial goals, but life goals as well. In this final chapter, I wish to help you teach your kids how to make goal setting a regular habit. I believe that this skill, above all else, will help your kids live more successful lives, financially and otherwise.

Setting goals gives a person confidence and adds excitement to our day-to-day existence. So have fun with your kids.

Why do I put such an emphasis on goal setting? Well, I have seen what happens when kids are not interested in their future. Lacking direction, they often become depressed. They exhibit a sense of hopelessness. Without a vision of an exciting and positive future, they do not care about themselves or other people. Kids without goals tend to dart from one activity to another, never spending adequate time on anything to get a sense of accomplishment. Teenagers who do not set goals for themselves tend to live only for today, never saving money or investing in their future. Hence, these kids may flounder for a long time before figuring out what they really want for their future and becoming successful citizens.

On the flip side, kids who set goals, and achieve them, see the world from a totally different perspective. They know that their futures will be positive. They know that they can achieve anything they want if they put their minds to it and work hard. They exude confidence and an aura of maturity.

By engaging in many different activities, and by testing themselves in many different situations, kids with goals know themselves better. They know what they like to do and what they are passionate about. They are well prepared to choose their own paths to a bright future. And finally, kids who know how to set goals are much more likely to achieve financial success. Always looking ahead, they save money rather than wasting it on superficial pleasures.

Kids with goals have clear ideas about where they want to go and what it will take for them to get there. In general they are able to defer immediate gratification and keep their eyes on future achievements and "payback."

If you want your kids to resemble the latter rather than the former, teach them how to set goals. Get them hooked on the habit, and you will be amazed at how they develop. The following guidelines will help you teach your kids to set goals.

The Key Goal Guidelines

Helping your kids set goals is an exciting process. It is my hope that parents will adopt and act upon these very simple guidelines alongside their children.

1. Encourage active dreaming

Every great achievement begins with a dream. So encourage your kids to talk about what they want to do in the future. Let them brainstorm out loud about all the terrific places they would like to visit, the kinds of jobs they would like to have, and the activities they would like to engage in. Do not judge their dreams or assess their practicality. Let them go wild with their ideas. Teach them to not be discouraged by those who belittle or disregard their dreams. Encourage your kids to make dreaming a regular part of life. Everything great starts with a dream.

2. Let your kids pick their own future

Most of us want our kids to be successful, and perhaps to fulfill some of the dreams we ourselves have been unable to achieve. This is a natural parenting instinct, but it is also a dangerous one. In most cases, our kids have different personalities, instincts, talents, and interests than we do. If we try to force them to follow a path of our choosing, they will end up discouraged, unhappy, and bitter. So let your kids pick their own future. Let them do it their way, not your way. Sure, you can offer advice and support. Of course you will! But keep it at arm's length. Allow them to participate in activities they wish to enjoy and learn from. As I have emphasized throughout this book, making allowances means letting your kids set their own course, with guidance from you.

REALITY CHECK ⇥

Talking to my boys while driving them to one of their many activities was a great opportunity to talk and ask questions. Little moments throughout the month allowed me to stay in touch with what was going on in their thoughts and in their lives. Now that they're on their own, we still keep in touch through regular phone calls, texts, and family dinners.

---

3. Expose your kids to lots of options

The more your kids know about the world, the more they will learn about themselves. To help your kids make good choices about their future, expose them to new people, new ideas, and plenty of new experiences. Talk with them about the jobs other people do. Encourage them to speak with friends and relatives about their jobs. Take them to factories and offices. If you know people who are successful in their work, have your kids meet them. Use them as role models. Talk to your kids about the lifestyle they would like to have and the cash flow needed to support that lifestyle. Also, encourage your kids to read books by successful and authoritative authors, including those in the Resources section at the back of this book. Most of all, let your children participate in an abundance of activities that interest them. The more they do, the more confident they will become.

4. Support the unique talents and passions of your children

If you see that your kids have a passion for a particular hobby or field of interest, offer as much support as possible for it. If they love doing something, that is likely the thing they should focus on. To help you discover your kids' unique talents and strengths, I encourage you to use one of the many excellent character profile indexes.

An index I have used with great success is one developed by Kathy Kolbe of Phoenix, Arizona (www.kolbe.com). The Kolbe Index, suitable for children at the fifth-grade reading level and up, will help you and your kids identify their unique instincts and help you direct them where their passions can make them truly successful and fulfilled.

5. Monitor progress and celebrate achievements

Perfectionism is one danger of setting goals. When people become goal oriented, they often forget to celebrate their achievements. They may be miserable, no matter what success they have had—for example, when they don't win, second or third place is not celebrated. To avoid this pitfall, help your kids learn to appreciate each step along the way. Talk with them about their progress. What accomplishments did they make today? How do they feel about it?

6. Provide opportunities and limits for activities

When your kids decide they want to pursue a hobby or an activity, lend your moral and financial support, with one major condition. If your child wants to learn how to play the guitar or take ballet lessons, she must be prepared to stick with the activity for at least one or two years. (You can agree together on a set time period.) She should not get in the habit of flitting from this to that, dropping out whenever an activity becomes too hard or too frustrating. So make the deal. If you are going to pay for her to learn judo or landscape painting, she has to sign on for the duration.

A great way to experience many activities without a long-term commitment or high cost is by taking classes through your local community center or college. Encourage your kids to try new things this way. The final decisions on how many activities to participate in, and how much the family can afford, will be made by the parents. But make sure your kids are able to give input. And keep the number of activities reasonable, based on the child's temperament as well as parental availability.

7. Talk about goal setting at the appropriate time

There is a right time, and a wrong time, to speak to your kids about their "future." Ideally, broach this subject when you are both relaxed and when there are not a lot of distractions. If you pick the wrong time, your kids might think you are pestering them. They might never get around to talking to you about their goals because they will think such a topic is not "cool." So use your good judgment. Pick your moments carefully.

8. Don't just set goals, teach goal-setting skills

You want to teach your kids how to set goals on their own, not just help them set some goals with your direction. This is an important distinction. Help them develop the habit of looking at their lives from a future-based perspective. Show them how to write down their goals and the actions required to achieve them. Teach them how to celebrate the achievement of their progress toward their long-term goals.

Worksheets and Exercises

Lifetime Goal Worksheet

Using the Lifetime Goal Worksheet (page 127) or something similar, have your kids write down the goals they want to achieve in their lives. Do they want to travel the world, own their own company, win an Academy Award, or have a big family? What other goals do they have? When they have these lifetime goals written down, work backwards. What goals do they need to have for the next three years, one year, one month? This exercise is excellent because it helps your kids see a direct path to their future. It instills the idea that even the biggest goals can be achieved one day at a time. Review these goals with your child quarterly, semiannually, and annually (or even as often as monthly with your teens).

Another fun and interesting activity is for your kids to describe their dreams and goals by making a poster, a collage of magazine clippings, a timeline, or a cartoon. This is a great activity for younger children or those with lower literacy levels. For the poster or collage, first gather together a range of appropriate magazines and brochures that the kids can cut and paste. Adults can benefit from this enjoyable visualization exercise as well.

Powerful Achievement Worksheet

Your kids can build confidence in a powerful way by listing their achievements on the Powerful Achievement Worksheet (page 128). Each night before bedtime, ask your children about one accomplishment or achievement they made that day, whatever that might be. Examples could include finishing a book, doing a good deed for someone, completing a chore the child hates, doing well in class, drawing a great picture, or having a good practice. Then have your children consider why the achievement was important and what further progress they want to make.

After the first month, start to write down their daily achievements in a journal. (Older kids can write the journal themselves.) Then after another month, together, write down two or three more achievements each night. This activity can be carried on indefinitely—or stopped and started over time. It might be especially useful at specific times in your child's life, such as when they are going through a personal crisis, starting a new school year, or making a particularly tough decision.

If you think that completing this exercise daily may be overdoing it, do it once a week, or perhaps from Sunday through Thursday, which is what we did in our family. After only a few weeks of recording their achievements, kids seem to look upon life with a more positive attitude and with a keen sense of achievement. This is really a simple exercise, and yet the results are remarkable. Try not to let your ideas about which achievements are important direct your child's answers. Listen to your child and learn—you will be surprised and encouraged.

Lifetime Goal Worksheet

Lifetime Dreams of

_____

_____

_____

Two-Year Dreams

_____

_____

_____

One-Year Dreams

_____

_____

_____

One-Month Dreams

_____

_____

_____

_____

Child

Date

Worksheet 9.1

Powerful Achievement Worksheet

SUNDAY	
Accomplishment / Achievement	
Why Was This Important?	
Can This Grow?	
MONDAY	
Accomplishment / Achievement	
Why Was This Important?	
Can This Grow?	
TUESDAY	
Accomplishment / Achievement	
Why Was This Important?	
Can This Grow?	
WEDNESDAY	
Accomplishment / Achievement	
Why Was This Important?	
Can This Grow?	
THURSDAY	
Accomplishment / Achievement	
Why Was This Important?	
Can This Grow?	
FRIDAY	
Accomplishment / Achievement	
Why Was This Important?	
Can This Grow?	
SATURDAY	
Accomplishment / Achievement	
Why Was This Important?	
Can This Grow?	

Worksheet 9.2

It's the Goal Setting, Not the Goals

When you are helping your children to set lifetime goals, remember that it is not important whether they achieve those exact goals. What is important is the confidence they develop from dreaming big dreams. Setting goals gives a person confidence and adds excitement to our day-to-day existence. So have fun with your kids. Don't worry so much about achieving every goal. Just enjoy taking the trip, no matter where the journey takes you and your kids.

Step-by-Step Summary

1. *Expose your kids to lots of different activities.*

   Get them involved in a variety of areas, including sports, music, theater, and other hobbies. The more they experience, the more they will learn about themselves.

2. *Complete a character profile index.*

   Help your children discover their unique talents and strengths by using an index such as the Kolbe Index (see page 123).

3. *Discuss the careers and life choices of friends and relatives.*

   Talk to your kids about what other people do for a living. Explain what the job is like, and what is good and bad about it. Talk about the type of lifestyle your friends and family enjoy, and talk about the education, training, or risks involved in making various choices about work.

4. *Offer your kids great books by great authors.*

   Reading is one of the best ways for children to explore new ideas and learn valuable lessons from the great masters.

See the Resources section for a list of books about financial literacy.

5. Do the lifetime goals exercise.

Using the Lifetime Goal Worksheet, ask your kids to write down the things they want to achieve in their lives. Then work backwards. Have them write down what they want to accomplish in two years, one year, and one month. Review these goals together regularly.

6. Do the powerful achievement exercise.

In this exercise, at the end of each day, your kids write down (or verbalize) what they accomplished during that day. They think about why each achievement was important and consider what further progress they want to make. This exercise helps solidify your children's sense of confidence and achievement.

Conclusion

TIME AND EXPERIENCE have shown us that money, or the lack of it, can be the root of much conflict in our lives. The debt trap is deep, so easy to sink into, and so hard to climb out of. Not having the proper education and structure to rely on can leave young people in a difficult position.

Recent news stories from far and wide have highlighted how young people are taking on record levels of personal debt, especially to fund their education. According to the British *Telegraph*, student debt in the European Union quadrupled from £42 million in 2008 to £167 million in 2010 and is expected to worsen. "Student loan debt exceeds credit card debt in USA" read the headline of a September 2010 article in *USA Today*. The article pegged student loan debt at $850 billion outstanding, compared to the $828 billion owed by consumers. "Oddly," reported Susan Tompor, "some students don't even know how much they owe— or to whom."

The situation is also worrisome in Canada, where tuition fees are not as steep. According to the *Financial Post*, almost 2 million Canadians had student loans in 2011, debt worth about $20 billion. David Molenhuis, chair of the Canadian Federation of Students, was quoted in the same article: "People are finding it more difficult to make payments, budgets are becoming more strained and we are seeing more reliance on food banks and the use of emergency bursaries offered by student unions."

At a time when economic growth has slowed, wages are relatively stagnant, and well-paying jobs are not a sure thing for college graduates, to be faced with large loan repayments is a daunting prospect for those new to the workforce. Yet your own children need not be among these statistics.

With parental support, education, and practical skills like the ones presented in this book, your children can become successful, financially responsible adults and avoid the pitfalls of lifetime debt. As you help your children learn to save and spend money wisely and develop positive, confident value systems (including a commitment to community involvement and a charitable lifestyle), you are sure to be proud of your efforts and delighted with the financially independent and successful young adults you launch into society.

Children need hope: hope that their future will be bright, hope that their lives will have meaning, hope that they can make a positive difference in their world. You can help give your children hope for the future. Make allowances for their mistakes, provide them with a solid foundation, and enjoy the great adventure as you raise your children to have both dollars and sense.

Resources

Books for Adults

Blue, Ron and Judy, and Jeremy White. *Your Kids Can Master Their Money: Fun Ways to Help Them Learn How.* Tyndale, 2006.

Gallo, Eileen, Jon J. Gallo, and Kevin J. Gallo. *Silver Spoon Kids: How Successful Parents Raise Responsible Children.* Contemporary Books, 2002.

Fay, Jim, and Kristan Leatherman. *Love and Logic Money-isms: Wise Words About Raising Money-Smart Kids.* Love and Logic Press, 2009.

Kiyosaki, Robert T. *Rich Dad, Poor Dad: What the Rich Teach Their Kids About Money—That the Poor and Middle Class Do Not!* Plata Publishing, 2011.

Pearl, Jayne A. *Kids and Money: Giving Them the Savvy to Succeed Financially.* Bloomberg Press, 1999.

Books for Children and Teens

Bochner, Arthur, Rose Bochner, and Adriane G. Berg. *The New Totally Awesome Money Book for Kids.* Newmarket Press, 2007.

Burkett, Larry, and Todd Temple. *Money Matters for Teens.* Moody Publishers, 2001.

Godfrey, Neale S., and Randy Verougstraete. *Ultimate Kids' Money Book.* Aladdin, 2002.

Graydon, Shari. *Made You Look: How Advertising Works and Why You Should Know.* Annick Press, 2003.

Harman, Hollis Page. *Money Sense for Kids* (2nd ed.). Barron's Educational Series, 2005.

Linecker, Adelia. *What Color Is Your Piggy Bank? Entrepreneurial Ideas for Self-Starting Kids.* Lobster Press, 2004.

McGillian, Jamie Kyle. *The Kids' Money Book: Earning * Saving * Spending * Investing * Donating.* Sterling, 2004.

McWhorter Sember, Brette. *The Everything Kids' Money Book: Earn It, Save It, and Watch It Grow!* Adams Media, 2008.

Games About Money

The following games will help you and your family put some of the ideas and goals in this book into practice in a relaxing and fun environment.

Acquire—ages 12+
Publisher: Wizards of the Coast, Hasbro, and Avalon Hill

Players invest in companies and their businesses grow and merge.

Careers—ages 8+
Publisher: Winning Moves

Players make choices to gain personal success.

The Game of Life—ages 10+
Publisher: Hasbro/Winning Moves. Also available in an iPhone app version.

Learn to dodge bad luck and make some money. Money is earned by doing good deeds, helping the community, or taking a break.

Making Cents Money Game—ages 5 to 8
Publisher: Lakeshore Learning

Teaches basic money skills. Children answer money questions and learn the value of each coin, how to count, and about gaining and losing money.

Monopoly—ages 8+
Publisher: Hasbro. Also available in an online version and as an iPhone app.

This classic board game teaches children about investments through buying and selling of property. Children also learn the value of money and about negotiating.

Payday—ages 8 to 12
Publisher: Hasbro/Winning Moves

A family game that makes family finances fun. Teaches children about the costs of running a household.

Risk—ages 10+
Publisher: Parker Brothers. Also available as an iPhone app and Xbox game.

Classic game of military engagement and world domination. Teaches about calculated risks. Helpful for learning about risk-taking versus playing it safe (just like the stock market versus savings accounts).

Stock Ticker—ages 9+
Publisher: Copp Clark Publishing

The object of the game is to buy and sell stocks and to earn more money than the other players.

Online Financial Resources

These websites are a good source of information on teaching children about money; some also offer helpful links to other sites.

About.com—Kids & Money
Teaching Kids with Money Games
http://kidmoney.about.com/od/teachingchildren/tp/Teaching-Kids-with-Money-Games.htm

"Play online money games, board games, or create your own home made games that encourage learning." Lots of inspiration here. Note that this corporate site features both advertisements and sponsored links.

Family Education.com—Money and Kids
http://life.familyeducation.com/money-and-kids/personal-finance/34481.html

A linked list of games and tips to help "teach your child the value of saving and spending wisely." Family Education.com is part of the Family Education Network, which has links to the international media company Pearson plc, among other companies. This site includes advertising.

It's My Life—Money

http://pbskids.org/itsmylife/money/index.html

Money is one of the six topic "channels" on It's My Life, a site for kids aged 9 to 12 sponsored by the Corporation for Public Broadcasting. "Babysitting," "Spending Smarts," and "Managing Money" are among the topics covered, and menu tabs link to games, video, advice, celebs, and a blog. Free of commercials.

Kids' Money

www.kidsmoney.org

This site describes itself as an "interactive resource for parents, teachers and kids designed to help children develop successful money management habits and become financially responsible adults." It includes a retail component, www.kidsmoneystore. com, selling print and audio books, videos, piggy banks, games, and other educational tools.

Money Instructor—Kids and Money

www.moneyinstructor.com/kids.asp

Just as it says: plenty of free resources, games, activities, and worksheets. Included on this site are printable "play money" pages—for educational purposes only, of course. Note to parents: sponsorship is unclear for this site, which includes advertising.

New York Times Magazine—Kids + Money

http://video.nytimes.com/video/2007/12/13/magazine/1194817108554/kids-money.html

A short documentary film by Lauren Greenfield about teens and how they spend their money in Los Angeles. Eye-opening but nonjudgmental, with the teens telling their own stories. An eight-page teacher's guide is available that includes a list of additional online resources for teens: www.hotdocs.ca/resources/images/uploads/KIDS+MONEY_EduPackage.pdf.

Humanitarian Organizations

For charitable giving especially when disaster strikes, the following organizations have a strong track record for their aid efforts in North America and overseas. Their websites feature up-to-date information on areas of the world where help is needed.

CARE International
www.care-international.org

A confederation of 12 national member organizations working together in more than 80 countries to end poverty.

Hope International
www.hopeinternational.org

This Christian faith-based nonprofit organization focuses on alleviating poverty through microenterprise development. It serves the poor in 16 countries, offering a sustainable alternative to short-term charity.

International Committee of the Red Cross
www.icrc.org/eng/

"An independent, neutral organization ensuring humanitarian protection and assistance for victims of war and armed violence."

International Rescue Committee
www.rescue.org/

Established in 1933 at the request of Albert Einstein, the IRC "responds to the world's worst humanitarian crises and helps people to survive and rebuild their lives." It operates in more than 40 countries and in 22 U.S. cities.

Oxfam International

www.oxfam.org

"An international confederation of 15 organizations working together in 98 countries and with partners and allies around the world to find lasting solutions to poverty and injustice."

UNICEF

www.unicef.org

International organization mandated by the United Nations "to advocate for the protection of children's rights, to help meet their basic needs and to expand their opportunities to reach their full potential."

World Vision Canada

www.worldvision.ca

This organization partners with communities, local governments, and churches in Canada and around the world to overcome challenges and to improve the well-being of children.

About the Author

PAUL W. LERMITTE is a certified financial planner who specializes in serving multi-generation families in business. In more than twenty-five years of advising clients, he has seen the subject of how to teach financial literacy to young people come up over and over again.

Knowing better than most people the impact that wise versus unwise money management has on a family's security and lifestyle, Paul, along with his wife, Jan, naturally wanted to teach their own children good money-management skills. Their efforts to guide their three young sons led to the *Allowances, Dollars & Sense* training system, which has since been tried, tested, and praised by untold numbers of families across North America. It works!

Paul is an enthusiastic, fun-loving people person who also takes family life very seriously. He works hard to help his clients through the many transitions and challenges that family businesses—and the families who rely on them for a living—go through. He is passionate about helping parents instill good money-management skills in their children from a young age, which led him to release a new edition of his popular self-help book.

Watch for future titles in this series geared to teens, young adults, and family businesses facing succession issues. Paul lives in Richmond, Canada, and regularly speaks on issues to do with money management and family business. Contact him at paul@paullermitte.com.

Index

Boldface page numbers indicate forms and worksheets.

Watch for these other titles in the
Family Finances series by Paul Lermitte

Dreams,
Dollars
&Sense

Strategies for Teaching
Your Teens About Money

ISBN: 978-0-9878076-3-2   Publication in Spring 2012

Decisions,
Dollars
&Sense

Helping Young Adults Chart
Their Financial Future

ISBN: 978-0-9878076-6-3   Publication in Spring 2013

A Legacy of
Dollars
&Sense

Expert Advice on Family
Business Succession Planning

ISBN: 978-0-9878076-9-4   Publication in Fall 2014

*For downloadable PDF files of worksheets
and more information, scan the code to the left
to visit* **www.paullermitte.com**